Leaving the Bucket

Searching for the Sacred in Addiction

by
Ralph Thurston

authorHOUSE™

1663 Liberty Drive, Suite 200
Bloomington, Indiana 47403
(800) 839-8640
www.AuthorHouse.com

This book is a work of non-fiction. Unless otherwise noted, the author and the publisher make no explicit guarantees as to the accuracy of the information contained in this book and in some cases, names of people and places have been altered to protect their privacy.

© 2005 Ralph Thurston. All Rights Reserved.

No part of this book may be reproduced, stored in a retrieval system, or transmitted by any means without the written permission of the author.

First published by AuthorHouse 09/20/05

ISBN: 1-4208-7488-8 (sc)

*Printed in the United States of America
Bloomington, Indiana*

This book is printed on acid-free paper.

Peripheries (Flinging a Cow) previously published in the New Delta Review.

Front cover courtesy of Deon Rossi. Copyright 2005.

www.bindweedfarm.com

Table of Contents

INTRODUCTION	vii
PLAINS	1
HYSTERESIS	15
WILD OATS	25
LETHEIA (HIDDENNESS)	31
BLACKOUTS, MEMORY AND NOISE	37
THE ART OF WAITING	50
PERIPHERIES (FLINGING A COW)	59
PLEACHING	71
SALTUS—LEAVING THE BUCKET	81
READING THE GRAIN	90
HUMOR AND EXILE: A RETURN TO DUTY	98
TOOLS (NO PUEDO)	111
RELATIVITY, CATHARSIS AND HORIZONS	124
HOW I SPENT MY CHRISTMAS VACATION	133
HABITS	156
PACKING FOR NAIVETE: A FORAY INTO THE CRIMINAL MIND	168
FIRST DREAMS AND MUSTARD SEEDS	190
BIBLIOGRAPHY	205

INTRODUCTION

The Tao that can be spoken of is not the Tao, reads a prominent line in the Tao Te Ching, yet the entirety of the book is indeed about the Tao, about something that *is* but which can't be explained. But the collection of essays you are now about to read is, unlike the Tao, about something that *isn't*—addiction—but which has been and can be written about exhaustively as though it indeed *is*.

Anthropologist Gregory Bateson said that there are no groups in nature, just minds which group things. Addiction is one of those things, a set of behaviors we can isolate in our minds but which upon close inspection has no real, identifiable borders. Still, even if addiction *isn't*, if we believe it *is* it can still affect us.

Bateson wrote about alcoholism in his powerful essay, *The Cybernetics of "Self": A Theory of Alcoholism*, in which he analyzed the experience of addiction and the effectiveness of the self-help group Alcoholics Anonymous. He saw addiction as a result of an imperfect way of knowing the world and the consequent being in that world, as a symptom of a problematic "style of sobriety," and he viewed AA as one way to sort out that epistemology-gone-awry.

Alcoholism is a way out of an intolerable normalcy—as are such disparate activities as shopping, sex, schizophrenia and religion. The following essays, underpinned in great part by Bateson's essay and other work, loosely follow my own internal and external experiences during years of weaving in and out of the oscillating process which we call life when we witness it on a large scale, addiction or alcoholism when we view it on a smaller one. You will find no answers or solutions in this book—for there is no real question and no real problem—but after reading it you may better understand a thing that *isn't*.

PLAINS

A lone pebble rests on a flattened plain. Wind arises, lifts and carries sand to the stone's lee. A dune forms and over time enlarges. As its size increases so does its power over the wind, which drops more and more of its load as it passes over. The more sand the wind deposits, the larger the dune becomes, reinforcing a cyclical action.

Elsewhere, on another plain, a hoof scratches the earth. Rain falls along the beast's path. A rivulet forms, cuts the earth deeper. The small furrow gathers yet more rain, and the rain deepens the gash further.

On a third, mental plain, one with few intellectual landmarks to demarcate its days, a tavern rises. A customer takes a drink, then another, and over years winds up as a chronic alcoholic.

A pebble, a hump, then a dune; a trickle, a stream, then a river; a drink, a habit, then alcoholism—we can call this *autocatalysm*, the process of self-generation.

**

The plain where I was reared had just one religion, one occupation, a single political party. The religion, Mormonism, prohibited drinking and smoking, discouraged sex and free thinking. The occupation, farming, moved along accepted technological lines, and those using different methods were ridiculed. As for local politics, I became acquainted with them in the 1962 elections, when a first grade friend asked my family's party affiliation. I didn't know so asked him what the difference was, and discovered a Republican goes to church. We were Democrats.

Singularity ruled every aspect of plains life and though differences occasionally emerged, they never notably altered its drab surface—strong winds erased them as soon as they rose.

The Snake River plain is known for such powerful wind. On most any summer morning it rises from the southwest by ten o'clock and by noon is a constant force. In the fall and spring, on the sandier soil of the Fort Hall Indian Reservation, the wind regularly blows out new seedings of wheat—sometimes three and four times before a calm and infrequent wet spell allows crops to take hold. The same wind sometimes buries the furrows of newly planted potatoes, exhuming the seed and exposing sprouts. Farmers then must wait for the first leaves' emergence before they can see to re-cultivate the rows. Though it might occur to an outsider to plant crops more appropriate to the soil, more able to withstand the wind, the plainspeople who farm the land do not think in terms of change.

In the winter the winds blow, too, following most snowstorms with a bitter cold that drives drifts across roads until they're impassable. In the still talked about winter of 1948 the snowbanks reached to the tops of telephone poles, and my parents, along with hundreds of others, were snowed in for weeks while supplies were brought in by air.

Leaving the Bucket

In the summer the grain fields bow to the wind, waves like the ocean's rolling through them. Sometimes the sprinkler lines miss an entire set, with the gusting wind pushing their fine mist to one side one day and to the other the next. If a hard wind blows when the barley nears ripeness the seeds shatter from their heads—every effort toward success is mediated in a like manner, at the whim of the valley's big winds.

Of those many winds, the strongest blows from Salt Lake City. Mormon dicta arising there erode any newness arising on the smoothened plain. When ratification of the equal rights amendment came up in the Idaho legislature, busses filled with protesters issued forth from church parking lots, heading to the state capital two hundred miles away to ensure that that the proposition fail. Blacks couldn't hold the church priesthood until a revelation from God arrived in the 1970's, coinciding with the building of a temple in Brazil, where more numerous shades of skin color make it difficult to distinguish in-groups from out.

Change comes only with difficulty to the plain, but even on this most featureless surface some ideas hold firm, and it is to their shadow side where windswept minds collect.

**

Our family lived at the river's edge, at the school district's fringe, just beyond the phone company's limits. It was 1973, when I was a high school senior, before we secured a telephone. Half-mile and mile increments separated area dwellings, and the closest oiled road was four miles away. Across the Snake River lay the Fort Hall Indian Reservation, off-limits to non-tribal members like us. Beyond that, the nearest city of size was twelve miles away as the crow flies, but thirty-five by car over the closest bridge. Five miles to the northwest a desert reclaimed its rights, sprawling for a hundred miles, a mile to the southeast the American Falls reservoir spread for twenty miles, sealing us from what minor civilization lay beyond. I passed many summers without seeing a single friend—my family was among the county's most isolated.

In such isolation I entertained myself by walking through the fields and wasteland. I picked mushrooms after infrequent rains, taking them to my mother. I found her sego lilies and wild onions until annoyance must have pressed heavily against the gratefulness she expressed. I followed my father as he baled hay, siccing the dog on field mice and counting snakes and other wildlife that emerged. In the evenings coyotes collected on the opposite river bank and sang, and sometimes we would watch the deer cross MacTucker Creek near the reservoir's edge. Even on an isolated plain, opportunities arise to explore; one merely has to adjust his scope of vision.

But while the plain seemed to sprawl forever, always there were the mountains far to the east. And on the sparse desert lying vast to the north a trio of buttes broke the vista. I could see the Tetons on the clearest mornings, and the Lemhis and the Lost River Range on rare occasions, despite their distances of over a hundred miles away. Without such points of reference the mind cannot calibrate its aim—the numerous mountains at the horizon's edge allowed me to discern my place in the physical plain, but I had no similar landmarks in the drab social desert.

**

The Mormon "word of wisdom" prohibits the use of alcohol, and I, though not Mormon, was intensely aware of that and other strictures. Despite the prohibition, in the nearby, unincorporated town of Pingree—with a population of just one hundred and fifty—in an area ninety-five percent Mormon, there was always a tavern on one corner or another.

I recall being a toddler at Gus's, having an ice cream cone as my father sipped an infrequent beer. A few years later I collected pop bottles on the highway after school, cashed them in at Joe's for a Nehi orange soda. Still later, after Joe's had moved to the depot across the road, I waited at Dee and Kay's for a ride home from afterschool activities.

I was fascinated by the pool hall atmosphere, its dim, yellow light and warm shadows. I liked the reflecting surfaces of glass and mirror and metal, and the corners and rugs that were allowed to collect a fine dust. The taverns possessed a type of men I was unaccustomed to but to whom I was subtly drawn, an easiness in them I saw in no one else. If I had to pinpoint their most prominent characteristic, on reflection it would have to be this: time, it seemed, did not matter to them, just as it did not matter to me.

Through my early school years I often heard of the evils of those who lurked at Joe's. There were tales of an upstairs whorehouse, drugs and other sinister dealings. Painted that picture, I experienced another—in my brushes with tavern life I saw difference, but not evil.

**

Without something akin to a thermostat, autocatalytic systems can become self-consuming, much like a grass fire out of control. A fire which does not stop, a cell which fails to cease growing, eventually overwhelm and destroy the parent system—limits, ends to growth, are as important as their beginnings. It's theorized that in a living cell a thermostatic device—an *inhibitor*—releases along with the "activator" that begins the life process, but diffuses more rapidly in order to check what would eventually be destructive cancer-like growth.

The rumors of tavern evils, the social equivalent of such an inhibitor, were no doubt meant to throttle the population's potential alcoholism and sinfulness. But, true to Hegelian dialectic, inhibitors become activators when opposed at a higher level—aware of the rumors' falsehood, I accepted them as their opposite, an impetus for a habit I would one day regret.

**

Joe Benini, the tavern owner whom the town remembers best, was stricken with polio at a young age. His legs rendered useless, he rode metal canes for most of his life, making his dark Italian arms among the valley's strongest. Behind the bar he kept a different set of canes, each fashioned from a petrified bull's penis and lacquered to a smooth finish. Joe raised a family via the tavern's meager earnings, earning the respect of even area teetotalers. I was late into adolescence when he died.

After his death the bar passed through several hands, most more suited to the buying side of the bar and all of them failing. The plains wind blew, the desert became flat again, though the old tavern stood the equivalent of three stories high.

The tavern was an abandoned railroad depot, bought cheaply in the fifties and dragged across a townsite road to a foundationless spot by the tracks. Built around 1914, it saw the days of promise when the brothers Pingree built an impressive hotel and store from indigenous lava rock. The brothers expected the town to become a way station in boom times, with the railroad just built and water soon on the way. They surveyed the town into lots to sell to speculators back east, but promise swiftly vanished, and the purchased lots now lie unmarked under farms and pastures, owners forgotten.

The depot then witnessed Prohibition, enough sugar passing through its ledger to serve an area many times Pingree's size, though perhaps not enough to fully service its stills. "Don't let your religion interfere with your business," an area saying goes, reflecting upon an ignored—but apparent—hypocrisy: many of the illegal distillers were supposedly teetotaling Mormons.

By the middle seventies, Joe's porch was sagging, its yellow Union Pacific paint was peeling, the shingles on its roof were gone awry. Kochia weed grew in the parking lot and around the building edges, and the wooden steps to the front door had splintered and broken. The religious no doubt imagined Mammon struck down, defeated.

Down the road a quarter mile stood a Mormon church, its architecture and intent sometimes mistaken for that of a bank. I spent a good deal of time at activities there with my Mormon friends, but never witnessed anything I might call God. The bus dropped us off at the church after school was out so we could attend Primary—a facsimile of Bible school—but I stopped attending when I learned from the same boy who'd provided my political education that it wasn't required.

Though I wasn't a church member, I was asked to play on the ward basketball team. No athlete, I was still a far better player than the local boys, and after several winning games was told I would have to attend church to continue playing. Knowing the demand unwarranted—in other wards non-Mormons played—I accepted the message as an expulsion.

I passed both the church and the bar every day on my way to high school, passed them every night when I returned. Together they framed my days, asked a dualistic question posed throughout my youth: would I accept religion or profligacy, God or the Devil.

A wind drops its load only when its energy dissipates, and a water current does similarly when it reaches stasis, the deltas of a flattened plain. I had stronger urges than could be quelled at Pingree's deltas.

**

A chicken, some scientists claim, is just an egg's way to make another egg. They see the human body as a conveyance for selfish genes wishing to reproduce themselves across generations. After high school, my genes would have settled for any like conveyance, but all the girls had left for city or college—the plains' singularity had left us with just one gender.

I was not alone in my desire. Those of us who, without promise, stayed, consequently headed to town bars and drink. We drowned our libido and wished for women, our misery settling for each others' company. On the rare occasions a female did appear, I was last in line to take her home.

I had a romantic notion absent in my companions, that love precedes sex. Though I was eager as they to get my stinger wet, I was thwarted by an ideal that had somehow skulked into my upbringing. I was a sterile plain, with the hard stone of romantic love embedded in my surface.

Every binge was a wind designed to destroy it. I drove to town, began drinking at noon, hoping to erase my annoying conscience. With enough drink I thought I might bypass my inhibitions, but most often desire was erased long before possibility arrived. The beers collected rapidly, covered the romantic pebble and the desire eroding it, my changed inner state behind it a bright new focus.

Ralph Thurston

**

By Christmas 1978, I had only by chance learned much of love, and was licking my wounds from a miserably failed relationship. On my routine way to town to drown the memory, I spied a light on at the depot—I pondered stopping by to see what transpired. Pushed from the city by my own inadequacies and shame, it took only a light at Joe's to pull me in—I had reached the pebble at the valley floor.

Ida, Joe Benini's daughter, was there that Christmas night, cleaning up her predecessors' mess. The plumbing had frozen and broken, the bar was filled with debris, there were empty bottles and full ashtrays left six months prior. But the jukebox worked and there was a sixpack left in the cooler, and she offered me a beer though she couldn't yet legally sell it.

As she mopped the dingy floor with water she'd carried from a neighboring home, I sat at the bar with a stub-neck Olympia bottle. Ida didn't know me but trusted me as I would discover she did all others, and she spoke to me as if I were a lifelong acquaintance. With each sip of beer and rural ambience I relaxed a little more, settling into a lifestyle I had first glimpsed as a child.

**

Other grains of sand blew in that winter night. A fertilizer truck driver and a farmer and an unemployed carpenter, all curiously drawn to the single light. Ida had charisma, a way of making us all immediate friends, and by the time the night was through we'd bonded with the aid of alcohol.

A pebble, a hump, a dune; a clique, a group, a clientele. As the winter progressed into summer the increased number of customers generated the coming of more. A car parked outside brought in other passersby, whose cars inspired yet more customers to stop. Friends of Ida's father, in their seventies now, came to reestablish tabs. Parachutists from Montana dropped in from the sky, eventually adopting Joe's as a sort of clubhouse. Lawyers and physicists stopped on their way back from goose hunting or river fishing. University students drove out from across the river. The local newspaper editor fell in love with both Ida and the lifestyle of Joe's, and quit his job before he was fired for having found a new attitude. Disparate people all, difference from the norm was their only commonality.

The hippies who collected about the tavern asked farmers for free rent in abandoned farmhouses; in exchange they made the homes liveable again. From one end of Crystal Springs road to the other, two and a half miles away, there were five houses in ten in which to find a spontaneous party. Within a ten mile radius of Joe's Bar, the ratio was oft repeated, as little rivulets of Dionysus spread across the plain.

Bikers and Mexicans and Indians and rednecks and hippies and oldtimers—normally at odds, at Joe's they gathered in harmony. T.T. reminisced of days on the flats in the early twenties while down the bar Clay recalled a recent acid trip. Old Pete thundered biblical passages against the wearing of long hair, I threw back my shoulder length mane and nodded. Ida catered to any who left a single difference outside: the difference that won't tolerate other differences.

**

Theorists of Complexity Science sometimes use a dune to explain the crux of their studies. These scientists equate perfect order with death and pure disorder with chaos, claim neither a wholly "plain" nor a fully chaotic state as desireable for living or non-living systems. For them, *criticality*—the point where a system nears collapse—epitomizes optimal success, what they call *fitness*, a term evolved from Darwinian Theory. The dune which can possess not a single grain more without collapsing is thus the fittest of all dunes.

At Joe's I studied complexity long before its time, trying to reach criticality each time I drank. I sat at the barstool and searched for the perfect drunk, where one gets the maximum high but retains consciousness. It was a process of great interest to a self observing itself, a self having lost all interest in anything else.

Frequently I drank alone, stared at familiar objects behind the bar. There were the bullprick canes, the freezer full of frosted mugs, an antique mirror, do-dads of the hopeful but inartistic. Bob Dylan sang from the jukebox in the corner, followed by Hank Williams Sr., Commander Cody, Yogi Yorgeson—songs linking my present to others' pasts.

The bar was inundated with artifacts: a camel saddle, an acrylic painting of a cowboy with a Robert Redford photo, a rusty toy truck from the thirties—anything that led to a story or at least a question. Together the objects formed a sense of bizarre wonder.

The wooden arch separating the main bar from the dance room had old cattle brands burned into its frame. I recognized most of the names written beneath each insignia, recalled hearing of most of the rest. Benches lined the walls, gleaned from other old depots abandoned along the railroad line, weaseled from the owners by Ida's charm and indefatigability. The bar where I sat, brought from a defunct tavern in town, had a different set of names carved into its surface.

It is easy belonging in a place of like minds, minds all in the process of evasion. I imagined I lived as the brand owners and graffiti artists had once lived, just in a different time, with similar problems and similar routes to avoid them. Juanita + Millard, I read, no doubt both dead now, but still alive in the bar's grimy etchings.

**

The Zen monk aims at a mind analogous to a dustless mirror. The restroom walls in Joe's, unlike those in most rural dives, were free of vulgar graffiti—was Joe's the Buddhist's no-mind free of dust?

I often stood at the toilet staring at the unmarred walls, craving a mind that could mimic nonexistence.

More alcohol was the closest I could get. One beer, five beers, drunkenness, ten beers, fifteen, unconsciousness: I lifted off the plain, and then fell.

Joe's and I, two pebbles on different barren plains, collecting histories to eclipse inevitable failures. Our futures any passing observer might have easily guessed correctly, but to us they were semi-obscured by hope. I would eventually bury romantic desire, Joe's would, like all Dionysian projects, see good times, then bad, and mine and others' alcoholism would end where all autocatalytic systems end without inhibitors: collapsed, to be leveled by howling winds.

We would become plains again, on which new differences might erupt. Cycles within larger cycles, every self and system plays out a process between the Dionysian and Apollonian poles, but the individual locked inside suffers a consciousness which inanimate units like taverns do not. Knowing change would eventually arise, I did not know when it would do so, and suspecting it would fail to do so in my lifetime solidified the alcoholic cycle—life on a plain is less tolerable when all horizons lie unbroken.

HYSTERESIS

T.T. whiles away his retirement like other area oldtimers, driving his old Chevy pickup to the store in Springfield, around the reservoir, back along the river and finally over to Joe's Bar in Pingree. There he nurses a cup of coffee for an hour or two as he trades gossip with whoever's dropped in. He remembers when Ida was "just so high" and when he exhausts the supply of new stories he returns to those shared from the past.

Having a spouse yet living, he is luckier than most of the older citizenry. Still, his wife works at the potato processing plant in Aberdeen so his trailer house is empty all day. When she retires she'll have the church in which to share time with the other old women, unlike the men here who, when they quit farming, lose their only touch with the community.

So, looking for a substitute for the mill, the tractor dealership and the hardware store, for the neighbors he once met at the head of the ditch or across the fence while working, he takes his daily route, hoping to find anything like the old days and different from his present ones, different enough to make a difference in the rest of his long drawn-out day. Week after month after year, his habit becomes more ingrained.

T.T. and I are not so dissimilar. I while away my disappearing youth as he does his golden years, my community gone like his. Just graduated from high school, I should be working or going to college, "doing something with my life", but instead I get drunk, get sober, get drunk again and again. My days are like T.T.'s in their sameness, being without friend or future, and month after month after month I repeat them drearily. If I stay in this rural community, my present will become my future, for there are few work or education or love opportunities. I will, as I age, do just as I do, get up late, hungover, drive past my partying companions' houses, perhaps to their jobsites, then to Joe's, where my route intertwines with T.T.'s.

**

Support a thin metal plate at a single point, pepper it with a fine powder, then stroke it on the edge with a fiddle bow; the resulting, unevenly distributed vibration will cause the powder to collect where amplitude is the least. The patterns that arise are called Chladni figures, after the nineteenth century Italian physicist who studied them. The plate can make many different patterns, depending on the bowing point, and is said to "remember" those which have been made, thus making them more easily produced in the future.

Joe's Bar and the surrounding community, like such a plate, remember the patterns first played out long ago. T.T., myself and others collect in the same ruts others have again and again since the area was first settled at the turn of the century.

The countryside remembers: The Gutting Saloon before the reservoir was filled, Chautauqua down in

Leaving the Bucket

Sterling at the Jungle Club; Art Nelson's place on the Springfield Lake, Vernon's 66 and Gus's on the corner in Pingree. The points upon which Dionysus placed and played the community platter have differed over the years, but his bow has remained true, the Chladni figures produced staying much the same. Drunkenness today is drunkenness yesterday, the drinkers differing only slightly, in perhaps no more than name.

**

The Gutting's bartender hauls the August ice from the pit, scrapes sawdust off its wet surface. Next winter they'll have to cut another batch from the lake, drag it over and re-pack it in the cellar. Sawdust, ice, sawdust, ice: the layers of insulation will keep the ice intact throughout the following summer.

They say Brigham Young, the early Mormon leader, sent one of his rebellious followers here to have his appendicitis cured by a resident "doctor." Supposedly on orders from Young's henchmen, he sewed a dirty rag inside the patient, quelling whatever apostasy might lay in store.

Old George is playing the punchcards at Art's again. At a penny a pop he'll spend a dime—unless he wins. He always orders "a shot of whiskey and a beer for a washer"—what we now call a chaser—and once served, hands the bartender a metal washer, always able to draw grins from the tired and well-worn joke.

Vanderford's potato warehouse workers are off at five. On Friday Ernie pays them and they stop off at

Ralph Thurston

Vern's for a beer and some pool, drink away paychecks and end up fighting—as is done all over the world.

Old Buss drives up to the bar with his horse—on a flatbed without sides, untethered. So well trained is the horse that he waits while Buss "gets likkered," then hauls him home drunk and asleep.

The drinkers' names differ but our ways are the same, all collecting where the noise is the loudest, all avoiding the silent grooves. Perhaps someday they'll tell stories of me and my day like they tell of T.T. and his.

**

Hawk-nosed and grizzle-faced, T.T. struggles on his cane to maneuver the rickety bar steps. He sits beside me, buys coffee for himself and a beer for me. He's had a pacemaker for nearly a decade, so avoids alcohol except at rare moments. I study his face for *prochronism*, the record of his evolution, but in the lines witness only my own projections. All is really know is that he's ending his daily route where I begin mine—in two hours he'll be home at supper with his wife and I'll be on my way to drunkenness.

Drunkenness is a route which I negotiate as T.T. does his, an arm out the window, looking, even praying, for something strange. Something, anything of interest to break the tired rhythm. A new face at the bar, a different idea expressed, anything to alter repetition. I play foosball, cards, dice, take a drive out to smoke a joint by the canal. When these tactics fail

Leaving the Bucket

I become animated, the drunken buffoon, make noise so I don't have to hear it.

**

Few great violinists allow amateurs to play their instrument, fearing it will remember the bad notes when played in the future. Over the years after Joe's death, many tried to play his tavern, but it responded only to Ida's bow. Her brother, two Minnesotans, a local parolee, a soon-to-be born-again minister—all tried to make a success of the tavern and all failed, but under Ida's tutelage it became a place defying logic, in a small Mormon community of less than two hundred drawing enough drinkers to drain fifty kegs in a weekend.

It didn't hurt that she was a woman, a counterpoint to the mostly male rurality, or that she very rarely drank. That she was hopeful amid hopelessness, doe-eyed beautiful and charming amid ugly vulgarity, did not hinder her success. And taking over just after the sixties, at the tail end of Dionysus' reign, allowed for her advantage. But no number of details used to describe her or the times or the community can explain her brief success at Joe's, which neither she nor the bar has since enjoyed.

It may have to do with thresholds, of how much repetition can be withstood before something new must be sought. Perhaps the old drum breaks when it has pounded the same beat too often. Or perhaps the countryside had long ago issued a question, which Ida answered when she re-opened the bar.

Nature asks such questions. A frog egg, while its head end is pre-determined from tail, doesn't know its right side from its left, and begins growth only when a sperm cell or even a pinprick breaks its surface, whence it proceeds, that break being the center of its bilateral symmetry. It asks, according to biologist Gregory Bateson, the question "Where do I start?" Pingree, waiting for newness, perhaps asked the same penetrating question.

Too insufficiently disciplined to be ascetics or monks, most of us clamor to the first pinprick of difference— points of intrusion being rarer in the country, rural residents are more inclined to seize them. We form our ways around life's gritty stigmata, like passersby gawking at accidents, and we haul the details to the rest of our lives, fill up the vast lonely spaces. Joe's became such a center, around which we grew our new being.

**

"You should fuck 'em all," T.T. says, nodding his greasy felt cowboy hat toward Ida behind the bar, "while you have the chance."

I nearly spit out my beer. "I mean it," he says almost angrily. "Or you'll regret it. You'll wish you had." I nod and laugh, but he does in fact mean it.

I wholly doubted his advice then, doubt it much less now. The ascetic can only be happy if he has a sufficient storehouse of memories, not the list of unseized opportunities which I had.

Leaving the Bucket

I laughed at T.T., thought myself wiser, more moral than he. Perhaps I was wiser—if I had indeed "fucked 'em all" I may simply have worn out more quickly. As it was, I extended my virginity longer than most, restrained the subsequent cynicism, as well.

A likeable but "malicious bastard", as some put it, he was always badmouthing someone—including, probably, me—but I never believed in his malice. He was just talking, filling space, trying to disturb the overwhelming sameness. I took his stories with several grains of salt, but listened, glad for even lies.

**

They say that Tommy, nearly eighty now, played in the big bands in the thirties. He still dresses exclusively in the suits in vogue then, whether it's hot, wet, dusty, or muddy. Dapper, white moustached and gentle, he seems as interested in us hippies as we are in him. Too old to drive safely, he rides up from his Sterling home—he is estranged from his wife in Utah—with a younger friend just out of prison, for a toke, a smoke and several beers. Occasionally he brings his sax and sits in with the local band, tries to merge with rock and roll.

He sits in the corner at our table, fumbling with the saxophone's mouthpiece while up at the bandstand Big Mitch plays his Stratocaster. Darrell, high on coke, is lost in his steel guitar, experimenting with sounds he's apparently never heard. Pablo bangs away self-absorbed at the drums while Randy sings "Fire on the Mountain." Tommy licks his lips, then purses them, breathes deeply and blows heavy into his horn, releasing a long, discordant note. I know they say how just a few years he could jam with the best, but either the music has changed or he has.

He tries to fit his sax in for two or three songs, but unable to wedge into the spacings he finally puts his instrument away and concentrates on his beer. At the breaks, passersby slap him on the back, and he nods and drinks without giving away his thoughts. I am embarrassed for him until he shows no embarrassment, and the discord passes.

Dionysus plays Pingree, Dionysus plays me: so why the discordant notes of my life? There are far more chances for disorder than order, more opportunities for cacophony than harmony.

We each have far too many players, as instruments we remember too much. Our parents, cultures, histories and spouses collide—we are fortunate for even a moment of assonance. Ignorant of other patterns, I might have once been satisfied in mine, but education and television teased me with enough choices to be haunted by the one I've been given. Choosing, said a sixth century Zen monk, is a sickness of the mind.

T.T. lost his work, Tommy his spouse, and I, my love: ideas. The farm, the wife, all meaning beyond reach, no one plays us now as we were played then— we long for what we no longer have.

**

Hysteresis is defined as the failure of a property once changed by an agent to return to its original value once that agent is removed. When I was twelve, my brother's college girlfriend left a copy of Herman Hesse's *Siddhartha* at our home. I devoured it at one sitting, never returning to my "original value." Struck by the events of the sixties, few of us ever did.

A number of Vietnam veterans frequent Joe's—those who joined or were drafted into the local National Guard, the nation's only unit sent to Vietnam, and those who evaded the draft via all possible deferments. Few of either type speak of the war, now just five years past, and fewer yet ask them of their experiences, knowing how dramatically they've changed.

Now they're back in the community they left, I assume trying to regain prior selves. But trying to forget only makes us remember more, leaves us chasing our tails.

**

Siddhartha found bliss after giving up desire, and a considerable wait which followed. He meditated, waited, extinguishing himself, seeking nirvana, an end to suffering. Bookish and passive, I was inspired by the character, so learned to wait, expecting reward.

I gained what seemed to me an infinite patience, then suddenly found myself with none, as I waited, then could not wait. I twisted Buddhist thought with the Christian idea that the good boy is rewarded. I became a vegetarian, gave up ambition, hurt nothing and no one; and I waited.

I waited mostly at the bar.

I wait for nirvana. T.T. waits, too, willing to settle for far less. Waiting for our deaths, we live, our two patterns combining to form a third, as Dionysus plays Ida playing us, weaving yet more lives together.

WILD OATS

Long, thin and light, the wild oat seed has a sharp tail as long as its body that attaches easily to passersby. Upon media as diverse as a pond of water or the hair upon one's arm, this little whisker can propel the seed like a sperm cell swimming or a praying mantis walking drunkenly. Thus, lofted by wind, via hitchhiking or self-propulsion, the wild oat proliferates, spreading its range at rates far greater than the fields of its relatives that it infests, the varieties of wheats and barleys bred for human purpose.

I sit at Joe's Bar contemplating sowing my wild oats. My fellow drinkers attach to the passing girls like oats or ticks, preparing to extend their genetic range. The girls, as eager as my friends to be bedded, don't seem to mind.

With fewer tools and less purpose than my counterparts, I have less luck—my libido insists as strongly as theirs, but my conscience rails far louder. On the rare, desperate nights I take home a companion to ease my loneliness, I wake feeling worse, not better. This is the mark of addictive behavior: an act which creates more need rather than lessening it.

I need no additional addictions—I have my own. I sit at the rural tavern today as every day, trying to transcend the life I'm born to. Listless, I run my finger along the counter, which Ida just recently salvaged from Ted's, the Indian bar in town. Jerry + Jozlyn, Ted + Gina—I scrape grime from the grooves of their ancient etchings. How many of these proclaimed loves survive intact, how many outlast their naming?

Other marks scar the bar. Over on the archway separating the main area from the dance floor, cattlemen have burned brands into the oak. Bothwell and McInihy, Houghland's, Bradley's, Edwards': ranchers leaving their marks like Ted and Gina, how many of *them* are still extant? Immortality is fleeting, perhaps so much so that we must leave something behind us. The wild oat self-sows, man stamps his name in the wood.

There is no graffiti in the restroom, no vulgar marks to scar what I assume must somehow be sacred. Why Ida inspires a respect absent for other tavern owners seems a mystery, but wholly apt. There is something different here, something ineffable. The Tao that can be spoken of is not the Tao, the wall which can be scribbled on is not a wall, has instead taken on a different form. Even Joe's bathroom wall can be bathed in the penumbra of reverence—by not owning, not marking, not demanding, we can touch God or feel His touch.

But the bathroom is not *just* sacred. During one of the Annual Barbecues held each May, an enterprising woman performed serial fellatio here. Ida truncated the event when she questioned the queue that extended out the door and beyond the pool table.

There were other vulgar acts. At the same wild barbecue, two men ascended the roof and mooned the hundreds below until a hosing with cold water brought them down. On another memorable occasion, the out-of-town parachutists laid their penises on the bar while the only female club member calmly marked the exposed genitalia with an inked Joe's Bar stamp.

What we deem profane would not have always meant "profane." The word stems from the common area which once surrounded sacred temples—an area not profane or vulgar in our terms, but simply surrounding that which the ancients deemed sacred. The profane acts at Joe's were less evil than simply errors encircling the sacred.

Such error is the detritus left along the path toward God—aiming for the sacred we're bound for failure. We search for God like the treebound tick, waiting for the passing mammal—when we sniff the telling butyric acid we leap, but most frequently we fall short of our reach—then we get up and try again. Error is profane not because we tried to near the sacred, but because we failed to reach it—the escapades at Joe's were less vulgar than misguided. It would be far more profane to have not tried.

We attempt the leap toward the sacred with a host of different ploys. Many use the sexual to find union—from the Hindu sect of Tantra to Solomon's Song in the Bible, the world's cultures abound with imagery simultaneously sacred and erotic. Others use intoxicants—*soma* for ancient Indians, peyote for Native Americans, drugs or alcohol for us moderns who lack the proper rituals to use them. There are those of us who use higher order talismans—love and truth and beauty—but even we are adherents of magic, seeking to manipulate the Gods through the skill with which we use our tools.

In *The Golden Bough*, Sir James Frazer distinguished magic from other religions by just this manipulation—those who actively seek to manipulate the sacred rather than approaching it with reverence are practicing magic and not religion. How many of us, though, don't reach for a tool to pry God from the place where we worship? Prayer, drugs, science—each can be used in a spiritual manner, each can be the technology of magic. Children pray for that certain gift, adults for love or release; I imbibe to invoke a higher reality, more frequently slip to a lower; the applied scientist discovers a pattern in nature which should inspire wonder, but instead exploits the sacred for human purpose—while the tools can be paths to a higher plane, we most generally use them profanely as magic talismans.

My preferred tool is the bottle, and sometimes with its use I succeed in experiencing the sacred. If, as Ida pours draughts, I slowly strip away all purpose, I edge closer to the sacred moment with each drink. I see my companions more clearly, feel the world more intensely, am able to discern pattern where there was none. But if I come to the bar intending to force my way to God, if instead of dropping my wishes I anticipate what may come, He evades me as if detesting my childish dependence.

The sacred is our way out of normalcy, out of our current context into another, higher one. Humor, ritual, art, violence, schizophrenia: all are what Gregory Bateson called *transcontextual* behaviors attempting to find that sacred place—life gives us binding paradoxes, the context of which must be broken to be transcended, and these behaviors can catapult us out of them.

But the sacred context resists the lengthy visit, evicting those of us who most want or need to stay.

**

Tall, wiry stemmed and loosely panicled, the wild oat lodges easily. It gathers, but cannot hold, the wind, and falls to the ground, flattened, particularly during storms or after heavy dews. Wild oats strip the area fields where spray pilots have missed their aim, strangling the wheat and the barley, bringing all down to share their demise. Avadex, Avenge, Assert, Hoelon, Fargo: over the years farmers have changed the chemicals used to kill the quickly evolving wild oats, which, becoming resistant to old tools, force the invention of new ones.

The wild oats stand taller than the wheat, hang their heads at wheel line height which makes the lines difficult to roll. Hungover, as usual, I attach the three horsepower motor to the line, and as it begins to roll pray it continues. If the oats wind around the drive shaft they will break it, or at best stop the worn out motor and stop the rolling line.

The motor sputters. Cursing, I shut it off, then walk down the line to cut the wiry oats, their stems so tough that metal breaks before they do. I tear at them with several slashes from a sheetrock knife, trudge back and start the recalcitrant motor; it stops several more times, and I repeat the process again and again, like Sisyphus. It normally takes me an hour to roll the twelve wheel lines one set, but on this final pass across the field it takes me seven.

The sacred evades us, evolving out of our control much as the wild oats adapt to chemicals. It is Hegelian nature, always turning our completed syntheses into new theses to be overturned. We wrench the sacred moment from the seamless world, but it flees once we think we have it. The sacred, like the wild oat, will live with us but not be captured, as it mockingly soughs above the field imbued with purpose.

Desiring sacrament, we would tame it, thinking we want only bread; desiring sustenance we might instead harvest the sacred, so capricious is its spirit, in such a seemingly incongruent place as a country tavern. The sacred may choke out the purposed, the purposeful can strangle the sacred, but our task is to cultivate both that they survive.

LETHEIA (HIDDENNESS)

It has been cool and rainy for several days—field mushroom weather, rare in our cold desert climate. My father and I drive out to Sainz's sheep sheds along Danielson Springs, one of the few mushroom hunting spots left.

With gunny sacks in hand, we walk the yards slowly, eyes searching the ground for differences in terrain. We avoid the area beneath the sheds—where there is too much straw no mushrooms grow, where too much manure, the same. And higher up the hill, where the ground lies bare and lacks both, the drainage is too great to maintain a necessary moisture. But midway between the sheds and the barren slope, where manure and straw appropriately mix, the conditions near a mushroom's deepest wishes.

As a field mushroom grows it lifts the soil above it, creating a bump on the ground's surface. When my search begins, every such lump is promise, but after numerous times bending to look beneath the mulch—and coming up with only a handful of sheep dung—I tether my anticipation.

The larger mushrooms are easy to spot, their white caps breaking through like a baby's head in birth. I scrape the manure away, cut the stem so the remaining spores are not disturbed. Some, spanning a hand's width, have opened to expose their gills. Once dirtied, these are difficult to clean. Older than the smaller mushrooms and tastier, they often harbor worms which make them unusable.

Still, we collect them, though we prefer those smaller clusters of buttons more difficult to find. Under the most subtle rises, these appear, but subtlety disguises in some cases nothing—Kierkegaard aptly wrote: never does reflection catch its prey so surely as when it makes its snare out of nothing. Eager to uncover the prized mushrooms, I dart from site to unsuccessful site. My brain addles. I become unable to distinguish between those rises hiding mushrooms and those covering nothing at all. Acquiring enough failure to dampen our enthusiasm, we cease searching, though no doubt missing thousands of mushrooms, still hidden.

**

Hindus believe God (Brahman) "hides" himself from himself in Maya, the world of illusion we know as the everyday. Alcoholics, addicts and chronic shoppers, searching for perfect binges and hidden bargains, play a similar form of hide-and-seek. They are involved in what Ken Wilber calls the Atman project. According to Wilber, I correctly intuit that God is in myself and want to find that Godliness, but because I fear the death of self entailed in that discovery and transcendence, I wrongly seek God—through the Atman Project (Atman being the part of God in the self)--in symbolic substitutes like sex, food, fame and power.

Leaving the Bucket

While hiding we experience terror; while searching we feel the hunter's allure. Both provide certain elation, so long as at bottom we understand ourselves as only in a game. But when we sense our plight is real—that we won't be found when we wish to be, will be found when we wish not to, will never find what we seek, or might find what we really wish not to—a deeper terror sets in, a terror of facing the impossible: that hiddenness *is* the truth, that there is no truth to be discovered.

**

Ed and I ride in his forty-eight Chevy, ritually taking the backroads down through Sterling. He passes a joint, I set my beer down between my legs, take a toke and hold the smoke in as long as I'm able. He pushes a new tape into the player, we listen and stare at the scenery. With nothing ahead in the day, save its inevitably turning toward night, we are slowly uncovering the world, gleaning whatever it offers.

We have no idea what will come. In twelve hours we may still be together, drunk at Joe's Bar, stoned out of our minds. Ed may find a woman—he often does—and slink off for an erotic interlude. There are dozens of homes I might end up in, passed out, a half-dozen towns where we might sample new bars, new friends, old habits.

We may experience a host of feelings. If we see Pat he'll accentuate Irish brotherhood—though I'm not Irish—giving hard handshakes, wrapping us in bear hugs. Colin may keep us in stitches with his wry humor. We may for a moment think we've found love, perhaps hatred, envy, jealousy, sorrow. Sufficiently sodden, I might end in tears—but only, I hope, if alone.

I drink for this mystery—perhaps all drinkers do—, having none in the everyday. Eventually I learn to find interest in the infinitesimals of common life, but at this stage of my life, when sober I see only dull repetition—the beautiful pattern connecting remains wholly hidden.

**

"And it only cost four dollars!" my father-in-law exclaims, having found a bargain at a garage sale, an item he'll never again use.

Not sharing his wonder, I'm uncertain what I should express—amazement at the object or his hunting ability, or commiseration that he's encumbered himself with another thing he doesn't need.

"The bargain" puzzles me. Is the bargain hunter a gatherer, uncovering the hidden, or is he an acquirer of coup, having outwaited the seller in economic battle—David slaying the Goliath of the mall? Is there the secret sense of having committed something taboo, a sexual arousal of sort, or does one derive a feel for the sinister, having cheated the storekeep but without having stolen?

William Barrett writes: "The Greek word we translate as "true" is *alethes* (literally, unhidden). This word does not speak of the correspondence between a statement and a fact... (but) only of something that has emerged from the hidden into the open." Though my father-in-law may be inspired by any number of less noble feelings, I suspect he harbors man's inherent wish for truth, to uncover the world. Unable, perhaps, to undertake the explicit philosopher's project, he instead exhibits his instinctual urge in the commercial realm Americans know best.

**

Near the first of May wild asparagus appears.

My father has a route for the hunt which begins along the reservoir. We drive into an old homestead, where only a lilac, a wild rose, an apple tree and his memory suggest people once dwelt. Having gleaned the several patches there, we drive along the old ditches of his boyhood, many of them now unused. He recalls every plant's position—there are two near the railroad tracks, some on the corner that swings by the gravel pits, one behind the tree on Vollmer road.

We are not the only hunters. Another gleaner has pulled down last year's growth to make this year's find more difficult—this dissuades the amateurs who need such evidence but not us, for my father remembers well. On weekends the pickers from town scatter through these backroads, so we pick on Tuesdays and Thursdays, beating them—and whoever has removed the old growth—to the find.

Quackgrass, already growing strong, disguises the young, tender shoots. At first I find the spears only with difficulty. But with each success my eye is trained further, and I race along fencelines, gathering, hunting, uncovering.

Barrett writes: "The Greeks did not have a word for 'true'. They had only a word that meant evident, manifest, open, present." Unable to find either Atman or the truth, or if at bottom we wish not to expose "the game", we may at least experience a semblance of the process of uncovering, exposing what has heretofore been hidden. In drunkenness, in shopping, in hunting for wild manna, we can feel ourselves revealing, practice the process of truth-finding, preparing us for a more enlightening day.

BLACKOUTS, MEMORY AND NOISE

Stranded on any landscape we need either some kind of shelter in which to huddle or something upon which to cling. We are reared to be contained from the outside world, kept secure first in cribs and playpens, then schools and finally careers. A few cultures take a different approach, raise their toddlers with a pole on which to hold, where they learn to walk and which they won't leave willingly until they grow much older. All save the most enlightened require a container or a tether, a background of security against which to experience their lives.

"Wise men see outlines and therefore must draw them," wrote William Blake—containers and tethers give our world outlines. Memory and imagination can be such vessels, as can a car, a tavern, a room or any arbitrary line used to shrink a background too vast for the moment. We may wallow in recall to escape from our present or future, their dreariness or overwhelming, frightening nature, and we may fall into daydream for like reasons. When these tactics fail we seek other available shelter—a habit, perhaps, around which to build our days. The most dear of these we call addictions.

Ralph Thurston

**

At night the farmyard lights spatter the darkness with a rhythm and spacing which almost exacts the stars. The sky drawn to ground, I drive through the widely spread constellations, by Edwards's and Stecklein's, along the desert's, then river's, edges. Pat reaches forward with a fifth of Jack Daniels, I pass a joint on to Colin. Lynyrd Skynyrd's music soars from the speakers, fills the minds already filled with alcohol, combines and lifts our spirits for at least a time. The car is a closed environment, a refuge sealing us from the world.

Stopping to urinate, we feel the crisp edge of night. The snow floor crunches as we walk the road's gravelly edge, collapses as we melt it with our streams. We write our names if our kidneys allow, seizing the chance to acceptably expose our genitals. An owl hoots overhead in the trees above McTucker Springs, flies as we look up, startled. The headlights, left on, capture fencepost, wire and sagebrush, some of the morning's frost still upon them some twelve hours later.

We drive on through the darkness, watch the posts go by, feel the railroad tracks running diagonally beneath us. We turn away from the main roads, stick close to the swamps and the reservoir, the saltgrass and Russian olives bent and still. Snow begins to fall, quiets even the sound of our wheels grinding against the frozen gravel roads. Somehow, despite the loud music, we sense this quiet.

Leaving the Bucket

Headlights and farm lights scatter across the glistening flakes, form penumbras of feeble effort against the night. I turn the windshield wipers on to give me a meager vision, switch the beams back and forth from high to low to see which aids me best. The gathering storm will keep yet more people home than is usual, giving us who own the night that much more room. At a break between songs, Pat suggests we return to the bar for more beer. In truth, we need a break, a different company.

I swerve around, head back. It's a quicker trip on the main highway, particularly when governed by purpose. A mile from Joe's we can see its yellow light, casting far out into the night. From this distance it seems serene, a single building calm amidst the snow and the dark, but inside we know it is as raucous as when we left it.

Pulling up into the lot we hear music blaring loudly. We see a group passing a pipe outside the door, a beer in every free hand. Through the window we can see another four men playing foosball, others at the pool table and bar. We finish the Jack Daniels, readied to join a larger aggregate.

We feel safe here, in a landscape without threat. The late hours keep the Mormon majority of the population homebound, the scarcity of traffic lessens the likelihood of police—the world is ours, if only for a few short hours.

**

We need beauty to live happily, need pattern to experience beauty. But we see an overly repetitive structure as ugly because it is too easy—we need to work at the act of seeing to fully enjoy it, must guess, not know, our life's pattern to appreciate it, or existential angst and boredom soon results. Entertainment is the food of depression, Gregory Bateson wrote, and art differs from entertainment in that one must work at it.

But a danger equal to excessive repetition lies in a life insufficiently patterned, its events too random or sparse to connect as beautiful. If we must work too hard to see, if we haven't sufficient information or structure to complete the pattern, we fall into anxiety or despair.

So one may turn to intoxicants when the world becomes too predictable, may become a user, too, if the world has no sense—if a way cannot be made through the confusion. But a drinker becomes an alcoholic, a user an addict, when the adopted pattern becomes given, when his days become like those he first sought to escape: ugly, unbroken, and entirely guessable.

**

I most remember winters at Joe's Bar. My dreary job as farm laborer has ended with the deep freezing of the earth in November, and no promise lies in sight— no work for months, no pleasure for, in my mind, a lifetime. For me, like many rural youth, all hope lies outside, in cities, in prosperous futures, in the arms of imagined beloveds, but I can neither negotiate city

Leaving the Bucket

ways—highways and traffic terrify me, and the notion of even moments in crowds repulses me—nor traverse the difficult terrain required for love.

My landscape is empty. The leaves are gone, the crops are in, the color has drained from the land. The elderly have drained their house pipes, winterized their homes and gone to Arizona—snowbirds in fifth wheels. The illegal Mexican laborers preceded them, went homeward on buses with purchases and belongings, all packed tightly in cardboard boxes wrapped with duct tape. The girls I shared years of school with have left for cities to find careers or husbands. One sees only the school bus, a few duck and goose hunters from Pocatello, or oldtimers like T.T. on their rounds through the backroads.

The winter is long and bland, the snow around Joe's parking lot high. Drifts roughly mark its edges, piled recklessly by a neighborly farmer's tractor and loader, and elsewhere rutted ice covers its rough gravel bottom. Only where I normally park, to the south side of the ramshackle entrance, can one see the bare autumn earth—measuring the extent of my drinking habit.

When a storm strikes, I stay for its duration—if I go home, I'll be snowed in, in the world I seek to escape. And when the snow falls after closing time my car usually remains—I have left with others to a satellite, after hour party. Noon to midnight, sometimes longer, Joe's is my home base.

Snowstorms break the winter's blue and cold monotony, with a dark, covering sky that shrinks the vastness. Though wind and severe cold will follow, returning the bland vista, these storms give us respite at least briefly. They are the catalyst for the most raucous nights at Joe's, customers rolling in with the clouds, sensing an imminent event.

They find the tavern cold. Built more than seventy years prior, only a thin airspace separates inside from outside wall. An inadequate gas heater hangs high in the corner above the pool table, blares full blast daylong even during warmer spells, with most of the heat either rising upstairs to Ida's and her two boys' apartment, or leaving through the uninsulated walls and windows. The furnace sucks away her money faster than customers can repay her, but nonetheless she tries to keep it raging.

The gas man comes almost weekly to refill the five hundred gallon tank outside. Finished, he sips coffee, trying to summon the courage to mention her bill. She flirts with him as he thinks about threatening her with disconnection, but the winter wears on, her good looks and nature stalling the act. Eventually a customer lends her money to pay the bill, knowing full well he won't be repaid.

On the nights of twenty and thirty below, some come dressed in their snowmobile suits, able to admit a habit most of us deny. They know they will stay until fully drunk, but the rest of us have to approach that state unintentionally.

But if it is cold inside the bar, outside it is far colder yet, and in lonely homes or unhappy ones it is even more bitter—in comparison the tavern seems safe and warm.

Leaving the Bucket

Bitterness—the tastebuds registering it rest at the roots of our tongues, as the last line of defense before we swallow, for many, though not all, poisonous substances are bitter, and our recognition of that sensation protects us from swallowing danger. But too much of anything is toxic, and while we savor the refuge of Joe's, taste its sweet enclosure, most us know we only mask the poison which eventually we must swallow.

Ida's morning coffee is bitter, too—less so, though, than the thoughts swirling from the nights prior. I force it down into my queasy system as the light streams in through the depot windows. Joe's, unlike most bars, makes no attempt to replicate the night—it is not from the day but from the world that we customers seek refuge.

I can see the school kids playing beyond the tracks and across the state highway, can watch the cars passing on their way to and from town. I can guess who'll be back and when by the time and direction they pass, and when they pull up in front I will have a greeting prepared.

They may have been to the liquor store in Blackfoot or scored a bag somewhere in Moreland. They might have stopped at the Crazies' house or over at LeeDel's or Toad's—the sites of activity which revolve around the bar being like whirlpools, swiftly erupting and as quickly dissipating.

The old poker table that sits by the bay window is covered with plants and potting soil. Ida and Randy are up on ladders, scraping decades of nicotine off the plaster ceiling. A few weeks ago they began stripping paint off the hardwood walls—there are triangular swatches of oak as proof. All tales of renewal, all tales of incompletion, but all tales of hope and future, at least—something which I don't share.

Dell lights another cigarette, filling the air with the too familiar scent. As the day progresses it will stain my shoulder length hair, my coat, my clothes, but I grow accustomed to it, even crave it, though I do not smoke, myself. The smell urges me to consider having a beer, but I wrestle with the urge, instead nurse the black coffee while we reflect upon last night.

I cannot recall the entire evening, accept the missing moments only with difficulty, startled by their absence. I grope through my mind for those shadowy parts which the others recollect. I fumble for their truth, until I feel the dim bitterness of shame.

According to Dell and Ida, I invented the "t-shirt trap" last night, heaving my shirt over girls' heads as they emerged from the lady's room. Familiar with my antics, Randy and Ida tolerated my drunkenness, but I'm still ashamed for causing them and others discomfort.

There are uncountable other, equally shaming moments I will accumulate through my years of drink: dances on the bar, a mudfight out back, throwing my shirt into the fireplace, dancing with chairs. I will fall through the front plate glass window, sleep on and beneath the pool table, be taken home often, too drunk to drive. Much I will not remember. An amputee, I will scratch at missing limbs, trying to reassemble what I've lost.

Leaving the Bucket

A pattern with pieces missing can often still be recognized—information theorists call this trait *redundancy*—but the pattern I call "me" doesn't include these humiliating events. I cannot contain the antics within the outlines I have constructed—codes can be broken, sequences recognized, but my fragmented self can't be rebuilt.

**

"When our vices abandon us, we flatter ourselves with the belief that it is we who are abandoning them," wrote T.S. Eliot. Alcoholics and other addicts leave their habits when the context about them changes. Though researchers have found that rats, in isolation, will choose to take drugs rather than food, they also have found that rats in a social setting with a varied environment will spurn them. Find love, God, or a good job—a tether, a container—and self-destructive habits seem less attractive.

Fifteen years beyond those years at Joe's, I am sober for some years and happily married. My three year old daughter and I are watching a black and white documentary on television, and she asks, "Is that what the world used to look like?" It takes me some moments to decipher what she means.

She recognizes the objects in the film—the cars, the buildings, the roads, the crowds—but thinks the world, not the tools used to record it, has acquired color since the film was made. So beautiful is her thought that I hesitate to explain, but finally I give her truth instead of beauty and reveal the secret.

This is my memory: black and white when unhoned, in living color when sharpened. I remember how alcohol elucidates the moment, still crave that heightened feeling of being, but I recall, as well, how it dulls the moment's concurrent recording, has left me full of blank frames, unassemblable, black and white. My vice has left me because my life is no longer just the present of the Dionysian moment—I need a sturdy past to cling to, an empire of self with which to confront the world and protect the family I love.

**

Coffee, cigarettes, beer—the day's textures progress once Dell suggests "a little hair of the dog." I watch the bubbles in the stub-neck bottle pass skyward and dissipate. I pull carefully at the label, challenged to remove it fully intact—this, the great effort of my day. I scrutinize the graffiti on the bar, watch the frost evaporate slowly from the bottle.

I have three beers down, another before me. Another and I'll be over the edge, too far to return to sobriety. I excuse myself to go to the restroom, ponder the last choice of the day.

The walls are without graffiti. Grime and hair hides behind the waterpipes which run lengthwise down the corner, and the door's lock hasn't worked for years, if ever. The music and noise of the bar is muted here, I am insulated for a moment from conversation and relationship. The room is small—perhaps three could move in it uneasily. The closeness mirrors my life. If I go home, the walls there will be more distant, but with that distance will taunt me with solitude. Out in the bar I can forget this, so the choice between the two seems easy. I smirk knowingly to the mirrorless wall. What comes ahead may be a fiction, but I intend to play it out in irony.

This is backstage, then, where I gather my lines, and as I urinate I reflect on the absurdity. I may not want to be here, but I've nowhere else to go—I just as well make the most of it. I may well end up unconscious; if not, it will only be because I exhausted all possibility, and, either depressed or having reached a strange lucidity, I will head home, to sleep off what I can.

I zip up my pants, re-enter the world.

We are creatures of many levels, ever-changing up the hierarchy of communication. The tavern is a refuge from the world, the restroom is a refuge from the tavern, but in the end I must return home, face the world at least in sleep, and when I wake, seek refuge again.

**

Gregory Bateson suggested that only through noise can new patterns arise. On mornings after binges, I seek a certain calm and silence, an escape from the noise of the prior nights, but instead gravitate to its opposite, the increased cacophony of the barlife I fear.

I seek a new pattern, for I find my life's rigid structure intolerable. I hide at home, teetotaling, with silence trying to break that pattern, then go to

Joe's seeking noise to do the same. For years I repeat the staccato rhythm called addiction, more vigorously, more quickly as time passes, hoping to break through the threshold which restrains me, but clinging to either silence or noise as my tool.

To cling happily we cannot know we cling, to be contained contentedly we cannot know we're contained, and already I am aware of my fearful clinging, containing habits. The alcoholic can cease drinking when he jumps above old patterns, stops holding to old habits and faces the world, but stopping, to me, seems impossible. Kierkegaard professed that we need correct measures of both possibility and necessity to avoid despair—I have neither, by my belief.

**

Heading to town in the morning, I find the terrain has lost last night's calm. The sunlight glaring on new snow overwhelms my senses. The road is slick, the night's snow compressed into strata now unrecognizable. In six miles I pass the snowplow and two other cars, forcing me to recognize other lives. It makes me nauseous.

I do not belong. I cannot compare to others. My attention on anything destroys it. There are just too many sensations, the dark background of my nightsky no longer a vivid, oddly illuminating contrast, my nervous system racing without alcohol's depressing effects.

Leaving the Bucket

I pull over at Joe's. Too afraid—of everything—I can go no farther. Inside, a cup of coffee and the ambience calms me, because I know this is the furthest I will go today, I have submitted to my fate and need not choose. I will get drunk again, return home to sleep, be sick tomorrow morning without promise. I cannot stand the threat of the open world, I need the dark covering sky, need to move from star to star in the long stretched night.

**

We leave our containers, we leave our poles, but through our lives retain our relationships with them. Twenty years later those of us who huddled at Joe's still cling, are still penned in AA, God or family—if not addiction. Some of us fear our old habits, have thrown them outside our containers, but others yet try to reconstruct what they once sought. Craving life as I experienced it at Joe's but trying to approach it without shortcut, I find myself contained, reaching for family. Having found one refuge, I still need another, from hope and love and the responsibilities entailed. My perspective spins, then, as it always did, but I deem it preferable to addiction because it is less repetitious, because rather than creating need it sates it. It is, in that way, complete.

THE ART OF WAITING

I do not remember waiting.

But I do recall a woman trying to calm me, a three year old, after what must have been a long wait. My pants pissed, I was bawling and screaming, with vomit on my chest and snot and tears on my cheeks. She reached through the car window, read my father's name off the registration that was strapped to the steering column, and went into the cattle auction to retrieve him so he could rescue me from what I assume was the terror of boredom or loneliness.

Though it serves as the background of much memory, we rarely remember waiting. Like the space between stars, the mat around a painting and the sleep surrounding wakefulness, it evades our attention even as it provides an unconscious standard for our focus. Dull as waiting may seem, we need it, for without such a backdrop we have no consciousness of foreground: the love, the award, the savior for which we abide have little meaning without an enveloping wait.

Aware of its importance, we may try to attend to the sheath of waiting which surrounds, but it then becomes the foreground, and we as easily miss the tree for the forest as the forest for the trees. Making a wait the heart of our attention, what we wait for slips unseen through our lives. Attending, then, to either background or fore, we seem doomed to lose the other to unconsciousness, but by situating our focus on both we can see instead what connects them, a pattern we might easily deem beautiful.

**

For twelve years I wait for the school bus each morning; wait, too, for the same bus to take me home in the evening. In the summer I wait for the mail to come, wait for the school's beginning in the fall. I wait outside the electrician's while my father trades man-talk, wait up on the bank of McTucker while he fishes. I wait for my mother at the fabric store, for the doctor and dentist in their offices.

I wait after basketball practice for my sister to pick me up, wait after games for my father to do the same. Sometimes, when I wait for hours in the cold and dark when misestimating an expected arrival, I walk the schoolgrounds, sit aboard parked busses, loiter on the dimly lit sidewalks.

Just as space surrounds my rural home—our nearest neighbors are a half-mile away, the nearest community six miles—a period of waiting wraps every event. Accustomed to this slow rate of unfolding, I learn to summon, even savor, patience. But when my will arises, I must also learn to endure the impatience arising with it.

In temporal space with well-defined ends, where hope and purpose are lacking, we can separate our lives from their normal flow of neuroses, desires and anxieties. Sometimes, we find freedom in the subsequent emptiness. After school, at a bar, at the edge of night in a parking lot, I find communion while waiting. I encounter friends who speak when otherwise they haven't or wouldn't, lovers among the otherwise indifferent. "A prisoner in solitary confinement," wrote Kierkegaard, "becomes very inventive, and a spider may furnish him with much entertainment." With sufficient background, the most minute details take on meaning deeper than those cloaked in excess. Waiting, we see what we would otherwise miss.

**

Like many sixties' children, I became superficially acquainted with Eastern religions. Filtering—and distorting—Buddhist doctrine through my Judaeo-Christian upbringing, I saw monks waiting for nirvana—so in willful and idealistic emulation, I waited.

After three hours of moving the morning sprinkler lines, I shower, drive twenty miles from farm to town. I park my Ford Maverick at Humpty's Dump, the local burger joint and teen hangout, and wait. The traffic goes by, cars entering the Dump, leaving. Eventually, a friend will come, or a stranger with whom to speak. I am optimistic—a magical encounter, a *satori* or a love sits just around the corner, and I wait faithfully, ready for that moment.

When the moment fails, I listen to eight track tapes—Neil Young, Lynyrd Skynyrd, Led Zeppelin—and, if no one comes, drive down to the beach, around town, and back. Again, and again, and again.

Then wait.

Leaving the Bucket

And wait.

And wait…

At three in the afternoon, I drive back home to move the evening pipes, then drive back to town again…and wait. The sun goes down. Stars appear. Traffic thickens. Other teenagers circle the Dump, flirting with chance. The stream of cars dwindles, then disappears when the bars close at one o'clock.

On occasion, at night's end deep into morning, having honored the universe in waiting by not demanding of it, I am given what I waited for. With all others sleeping, the world becomes wholly mine. It is a world difficult to describe, for to pull out a piece removes the wholeness it has, the quality for which I wait all day, all summer, for which I will wait all my life.

The dayworkers have passed by on their way home from jobs. The nightcrowd left hours ago, having decided there was nothing left to gain. Even the most desperate have gone home in need, unable to face the town's emptiness. *Samsara*, the birth and death of things, seems removed—or, if not removed, unjudgeable, the world for once seeming precisely as it should be. I imagine this sense of fullness as God's permanent state of being, and only by returning to the impulses rising from self do I lose it.

Tired, I drive home, move from waiting to sleep.

**

Gregory Bateson suggested that rather than count our fingers, we should count the gaps between them.

For him, the patterns which connect were every bit as real as the things they unite. The gap and the finger, to Bateson, comprised the system or pattern that should be the base of our attention—gap-and-finger, and how they relate to one another.

A zebra's white stripes are as necessary as the black ones, the space between quantum leaps as important as the electrons making them. Perhaps, then, we should focus on the waiting in our lives as much as those events we normally consider important. And then, after having witnessed both white stripes and black, see the pattern which is both, see beauty.

**

Some nights I park at the cemetery, just a mile from the home of a girl with whom I'm infatuated— if fate is kind, she will see me and stop. Every car light approaching from Blackfoot fills the night with promise. Minutes pass between cars as I lie on the hood in the warm summer air hanging still. At last, one turns from the highway, down the gravel—perhaps it is her, perhaps she'll see me, return.

But the taillights pass into the darkness.

Midnight, one o'clock, two, the highway deadens as my patience deepens. I am of course in love with love, not her, and tired, I at last go home, my will and love strengthened in my imagination.

I will spend much of a summer loving distantly just this way—the beloved never knowing. I am able to bask in imagined amorous scenes, damned

Leaving the Bucket

to experience rejection, too, an entire life of romance taking place, but only in my mind.

Throughout Samuel Beckett's famous work, *Waiting for Godot,* Estragon and Vladimir wait for the unknown Godot, who, though by messenger promising to come, never does. The two are bored by the tedium, driven to distraction, buried in trivial discussion and argument as they wait, and wait, and wait. Meant as a bleak and bitter parallel to man's hopeless existence, it perhaps inadvertently expresses the deleteriousness of both purpose and passivity.

Passively waiting for Godot or a girl we imagine we love, we pull at the world, wasting our energies, neurotics creating vacuum with need and desire. Waiting for Godot, Estragon and Vladimir waste away in triviality, their purpose paradoxically creating their aimlessness. Without Godot, they might attend to their lives, to helping others (which waiting, they fail to do), and be happy doing so.

If we want, we should actively seek, not wait for but meet our desire, but then, having purpose, we anticipate, expect, or demand—wait as children, not the artists we are.

**

I sit at Joe's Bar, spin the drink in my hand—I am waiting for figure to appear. A safecracker with fingertips sanded (*patience, ease into the moment*), I caress the day's tumblers rolling ready (*sensitivity— know where the world meanders*). I need the confidence of a believer, an acrobat's balance, the reverence of a priest toward his savior.

I must assimilate any external or internal annoyance, or lose the feel of the space I'm exploring. To wait so requires a tightrope walker's balance, which paradoxically requires constant imbalance. The walker's pole and body are never still, but in motion, changing slightly to lessen a more dramatic change which might cause him to fall. Moving with but minor purpose, he deflects nature's whimsical laws.

It's said that the neurotic makes the world come to him, that the psychotic presses himself on the world. Strung between those behavioral poles hangs a spectrum of action, a rope with an uncertain degree of tension. Toward the slack center, one needs greater presence and better balance, while near the ends one's mistakes may be forgiven. He who hesitates may fall, but so does the one who acts prematurely—those waiting artfully stay aloft.

I order another, drink deeply, and wait.

**

Early to a matinee I sit alone in the theatre, framing the coming event. I expand through the space, to empty seats and aisles, surround what will come with what is. If I shed what I've brought I'll not tarnish what may follow.

The best art inspires catharsis, an act of purification. Properly experienced, a movie, a book, a play or a wait can bring to consciousness and heal a buried psychological complex. But, too close to the action in a play we feel only emotion, while too distant we experience only our critical faculties. But balanced between, we merge the two senses, are lifted above normal experience and into a new realm.

Not so fortunate today, I watch the credits roll as the movie ends, let the lights lift the other viewers from their seats. When the ushers walk in to survey the aisles for trash or stowaways, I leave, the movie framed symmetrically by my lingering, at least honored with waiting.

**

Living at the desert's edge, attempting a painful asceticism, I sit outside my cinderblock dwelling, wait for the summer's daily storm to roll in. The afternoon thunderhead rises, all viciousness and heat, aimed apparently for me. Loveless, jobless, without future, I can see no possibility. Nor can I bask in a golden past. The lightning strikes along the horizon, thunder breaks the air about me. Aching with loss, impotently railing at a malignant sky, I edge toward self-annihilation.

Suddenly a coyote bursts from the field, runs through the yard just a few feet away. As swiftly a hawk swoops down within inches of the coyote's back, pecking at it in chase—and laughs, its cackle not bird but human.

A hard and sharp cuff to my ears, the scene knocks loose my self-pity. Laughing, the hawk follows the coyote from sight. Rain follows, the storm punctured by change.

**

"Men," wrote Kierkegaard, "are divided into two great classes: those who predominantly live in hope, and those who predominantly live in recollection. Both have a wrong relation to time. The healthy individual lives at once both in hope and in recollection, and only thereby does his life acquire true and substantial continuity."

According to a Zen adage, the sage eats when hungry, sleeps when tired. When, then, does he wait?

Seize the day.

PERIPHERIES (FLINGING A COW)

The Mexican laborers and I have joked for years now about me marrying Margarito's sister-in-law, Celestina. "*Muy bonita*," says Chon, grinning lecherously while I gas up the trucks. He pokes his index finger back and forth through the enclosed circle of his other hand's thumb and forefinger. "*Bueno for cojer.*" I respond with my own vulgar gestures, in bastardized Spanish intimate that masturbation will do.

Up until now such repartee has sufficed, but this year Margarito presses more earnestly. "You need wife," he tells me as we ride out to the tractors. "She doesn't speak English," I say, to which Margarito replies, "No need talk. Better no talk—no fight." I laugh, but he is serious.

**

It is the year of the grasshopper. Government warplanes, fitted with spray equipment, drop tons of insecticide where the desert's edge meets farm ground, in broad swaths totaling hundreds of thousands of acres. As they have approximately every twenty years for the last century—when the spring rains fail and allow their eggs to develop without disease--, the hoppers come in swarms from the dry, unpalatable junegrass and sagebrush to gnaw at the fresh green of potatoes, beets, hay and grain. In swaying ribbons that swing fifty, a hundred, then two hundred feet past fencelines and into fields, they cut every stalk of tender foliage to the ground. We see multitudes on the highway bordering the field, some dying, some dead, their bodies crushed where pickups have broken their paths.

Technically, we shouldn't be out here so soon after spraying, but with only a twenty-four hour residue, Malathion seems safe compared to the other chemicals we use. We get out of the truck to check if the spray was effective, see at least some of the grasshoppers staggeringly answer our question.

**

Every time I pick up Margarito to head out to move pipes, it's the same: "When you marry Celestina?"—my laugh is insufficient reply. "Can she cook?" I ask. "No need," he says. "Can she clean?" I ask. "No need." "No cook, no clean, no bueno," I say, but he replies, "Si, bueno for Ralph. Better'n drinkin'. Ralph drink too much. Ralph have wife, Ralph no drink."

He's right, but I change the subject. I ask if it's papers she wants, so she can stay in the U.S. legally—anyone married to an American citizen becomes legal. "She want Ralph," he says. "She doesn't even know me," I insist, but Margarito will have none of it. "You go bar, Saturday. You ask."

Deeper into misunderstanding, I am tired of fending him off, always giving more ground. Okay, I say, relenting, you go to the bar on Saturday and bring Celestina. He nods, smiles, lifts his shoulders as though victorious, then shrugs, ready to assume a new burden.

Maybe our tiresome routine will end then, I think. On the other hand, I add wryly, the available women are so few that I just may take a wife with whom I cannot speak.

**

Ben, my three year old nephew, rides behind me on the four-wheeler. Down the highway we drive, up the spud cellar road and across the lateral canal, onto the path that parallels its bumpy bank. The sprinklers water the path through the summer, giving rise to a good crop of weeds which rub alongside us as we drive.

Stirred by the four-wheeler's noise and movement, thousands of grasshoppers jump from the undergrowth. They fly every which way across the canal, beneath us, across our path—a few, unlucky, strike us. Ben stiffens and begins screaming as loud as he can. I slow down and try to calm him, but he implores me to speed back up: yelling, he shouts, makes him less afraid. By screaming, apparently, he can pay attention to himself rather than the insects.

Only three, Ben unconsciously knows what Sartre posited a half century ago: that we can be either subjects or objects, but not both. As subjects, Sartre claimed, we might turn our gaze upon others, see them merely as objects, or vice-versa, instead experience ourselves as objects, under their subjective gaze. We can thus never be truly united with another, nor experience life simultaneously as both active and passive.

All the way back from the pump Ben yells, protecting himself not only from the invasive gaze of the world outside but from his own.

**

Roy Rappaport writes: "In an unpredictably changing universe, it is a good evolutionary strategy... to give up as little flexibility as possible, to change no more than necessary." Is it true, then, that in an unchanging world such as I circulate in, one should change as much as possible—use that potential of flexibility—in order to survive?

Every drunken binge is intended to inspire such massive change; instead it reifies what is. Contexts oft repeated become drudgery, even frightening, and I fear I will always be doing this: driving tractors and trucks in a sterile rural life, spending weekends in the bar, weekdays feeling ill, without a mate or a friend with whom to share my life.

During binges I forget all this. With a narrowed scope, anything seems possible, and most any variation is welcome. A new kind of beer, a new face, seem through the framework of intoxicants to be new contexts, but awakening from a long delirium I find them not new at all—I have moved my furniture around, but I remain in the same house.

"Man perpetuates tradition even in those institutions that attempt to flaunt it," wrote anthropologist

Leaving the Bucket

Ruth Benedict, addressing the Dionysian nature of most American Indian tribes. When the urge toward strong or violent experience, which stems from a need to break everyday life, itself becomes commonplace, how does one get beyond, into the freeing context of the sacred?

**

She's beautiful, grins shyly from across the table with eyes downturned as I speak to her. She doesn't understand my poor version of Spanish, nor I her rapid—but equally incoherent—variety, so I speak to Margarito and he translates what I say—hopefully, with accuracy. As he interprets Celestina's reply to me, his wife, Esperanza, speaks with her. I try to listen to both conversations, but the women speak so swiftly that their words are indecipherable.

I ask her the necessary questions, looking for solution to satisfy us both: why do you want to get married? You need papers?—I am willing to marry for that reason, I tell Margarito, she doesn't need to live with me. We can live together for a few months, then divorce, and she'll have what she wants.

But she wants to live with me.

Do you want children?—I don't want children, I tell Margarito.

She doesn't have to have children, either, he says, adding: "Ralph want, not know Ralph want."

Don't you need to be in love?

Margarito doesn't even ask her this. Mexicanas don't need love. "Not same like Americanas," he says. "No need."

Ralph Thurston

She just answers yes to everything and smiles. Information is a difference that makes a difference, wrote Gregory Bateson, but since her answers do not differ, they convey little information.

Margarito insists on buying more beers. I drink rapidly, trying to extract myself from what is becoming an inextricable situation. As Margarito and his wife join the other Mexicans in a circular dance that rotates the whole of the floor, I try to talk to Celestina, but she just smiles.

Why not? I ask myself, shrugging through the thumping Latin music and sawing noise of the accordion. I look at her white teeth, bronze body, flawless smile, flowing hair—she is beautiful in black heels, tight levis, and a white blouse with just enough cleavage: she's learned her wiles well. And my lust is great, coloring my judgment. Who am I protecting?—if she wants to marry someone she doesn't know, that's her business.

Okay, I say to Margarito when he gets back to the table, we can get married.

**

In one medieval battle during which a castle lay under siege of another kingdom, a stalemate was reached because of the impenetrability of the defender's walls and position on much higher ground. The defenders couldn't leave, but their enemies couldn't advance. Intending to wait out the besieged, the enemy camped out, expecting starvation to eventually open the gates to victory.

Leaving the Bucket

The defenders held out, and the enemy wore down, both sides' hopes increasingly dashed as the months wore on. Day after day after day the stalemate continued, until the storehouse of the castle—unbeknownst to the enemy—was down to the last cow and final sack of grain. The king ordered the cow killed and the grain stuffed in its carcass, then had his men fling it over the castle walls and into the enemy camp.

Disheartened by the gesture, the apparent abundance still in the castle's holdings, the enemy packed up and left, their task of waiting for victory now seeming impossible.

When two factions—of any sort, be it ideas, people, or behaviors—grapple in a stalemate with no promise of end, only the wholly unexpected can break the context which maintains it. "Flinging a cow" lifts the dialogue between the foes to a different, more creative level where change or even synthesis can occur.

Trapped in such a dialogue which I cannot escape, between sobriety and drunkenness, idleness and overworking, I contemplate a similar act. Maybe, just maybe, marrying a stranger with whom I cannot speak can change the redundant and addictive dialectic that has become my life.

**

At closing time we all walk from the bar and around the cellar to Margarito's tiny home, once a government trailer hauled in to temporarily house those who lost their homes in the Teton Dam collapse in the mid-seventies. Inside, there is still food from an earlier supper on the grease riddled stove. Chon turns on a burner and begins stirring the indiscernible but fragrant mixture.

The four children are asleep in one room—Celestina sleeps with them, while Margarito and Esperanza share the end room. Chon and Faustino have the tiny room between them, and the nephews, Roberto and Juan, sleep on the dirty carpet of the living room floor. I am humbled by the squalor.

Margarito spoons out burritos to us all, opens beers. Chon, Faustino, Chuy and I sit at the table while the sisters stand against the trailer wall. Chuy gives congratulations after Margarito speaks with him, and I look to Celestina's face but derive no meaning.

As I wolf down a burrito, Margarito tries to make arrangements for the wedding. I am careful to resist one last time; I want to have her alone, try once more to see what she really wants. Through two beers we dicker and laugh, the atmosphere jubilant, drunken and ignorant. Finally, Margarito clears the room, Faustino and Chon making suggestive comments, as all go to bed but Celestina and me.

**

I make the move any man makes, though less deftly. Celestina and I exchange lips and tongues, but she meets further reaches with resistance—she's not as eager as Margarito claimed. I have brought a Spanish-English pocket dictionary, hoping to elicit understanding, and thumb through the pages between beer-sodden kisses. *Beso*—kiss. I rifle through the tiny pages and hold them to the dim light. *Tocar*—touch.

Leaving the Bucket

I look for a word for love, but unsuccessful, guess at a Latin root. *Amore*—no response. Amo. Amer. She doesn't seem to understand what I try to say.

Though she's avid enough in my embrace, I feel little emotion—not even lust. If she wished me to perform I probably couldn't. My mind hovers outside us both, considering the situation, appraising it as absurd but still of interest. More pathetic than ironic, less tragic than merely asinine, it illustrates how ill-fitting my world has become.

I ask to go to her room. Smiling as always, she changes my meaning, says it's okay to sleep with the children. No, I say, *contigo*—with you. She just repeats her first reply—we are as man and dolphin, communicating in a narrow sonic range that only rarely overlaps. For an hour I have my efforts thwarted, finally head to the floor to sleep by Roberto and Juan.

**

Hungover, I pick her up the next Saturday, intent on living by my word—it wouldn't be the first time I committed happily to something when drunk and then, sober, wished I hadn't.

We drive to the mall in Pocatello, I ask her if she wants to go shopping, watch the skateboard competition out front—she just smiles and acts nervous, which I interpret as a "no". I drive to the zoo, we stroll past the cages, but, wearing high heels, she finds walking difficult. I drive on to the mountains, thinking she might like scenery, park and find a spot to sit down. She follows me, I try to touch her, she recoils—apparently *that's* not on her mind.

Exasperated, out of ideas, I suddenly realize my foolishness. Though perhaps able to live with someone who doesn't share my language, I cannot live with one with whom I can't communicate. Relieved, I start for home, no longer incessantly trying to elicit her answers.

Arriving in American Falls, almost home, Celestina finally attempts to say something. Excited now, she wants to stop at a café and get something to eat.

"No," I say. "We're going home." I savor my sudden resolve.

**

I am the periphery, the desert's edge, where Mexican national meets American society. Such desert ecology lacks the diversity seen in less harsh climates and places, has fewer species, a more easily penetrated network. Like islands, where whole classes of life may be missing—mammals, predators, reptiles--, the desert, while appearing stable and unchanging, is easily disrupted. A single predator, introduced where before they were unknown, can extinguish whole species in a very short time.

At the shoreline, at the desert's edge, here at the fringe of society, intrusions begin which are crucial to the success of either the invader or the invaded. Was I being "invaded?"—I cannot assess Celestina's authenticity. Was Margarito doing me a favor, or trying to extract one from me?—who can judge the meaning of communication between different groups?

Leaving the Bucket

It may be only that chance boundaries were meeting, ripe for some sort of change.

Change occurs as borders shift, as entities exchange information; but if only meaningless details move across the border, no context can be even minusculely altered.

**

Two years later it is the year of the jackrabbit. On Wulf's place, the furthest out on the desert, they swarm in droves of thousands. As spotlights cross their undulations, they simulate ocean waves—eroding the shore where farm meets high plains desert. Hunters ride in jeeps with automatic rifles set in turrets, riddle the ocean with malice but with no apparent effect. But in the morning when the tide has receded, the dead number well over a thousand, and carrion-birds flock to the frozen carcasses.

Starved because of their vast numbers and the insufficient food supply of the desert, the rabbits come into the farmers' haystacks, eat at their bases until the stacks collapse, unsupported. Worse, they defecate in the hay, destroying far more than they eat. Further north, in Mud Lake, the farmers have a round-up, stretch their numbers across the desert to drive the rabbits into pens where they then club them to death. It does little good, but it extinguishes for a moment a feeling of helplessness.

Only those at the periphery, where desert meets farm, feel the true brunt of the migration, but many more wish to join and experience the carnage. Making barbarism out of what might be deemed necessity, they make the national news for playing "bunny ball" with baseball bats.

Eventually, when wet weather comes, a disease will strike the jacks, diminish their numbers for another twenty year cycle without any effort by the farmers. It seems what happens, happens, no matter what our efforts—and what doesn't happen, doesn't, no matter the lack of trying.

I sit at the bar listening to the farmers complain, contemplate how nothing changes: grasshoppers one year, antelope and rabbits another, something always presses against every effort, threatening sameness with change and change with sameness.

Celestina, as yet unmarried, nonetheless has a son by another American. Legalized now, she draws support from the state welfare system—perhaps what she wanted in the first place. I still drive tractor or truck from March into November, still drink in four day thrusts against my context. Having refrained from one foolish decision, I have yet to exercise my evolutionary flexibility—I still know that someday I shall have to fling a cow.

PLEACHING

Sitting in on Alcoholics Anonymous meetings for a graduate sociology paper, I confront my past, observing not just strangers emerging from society's dregs but cohorts from my own drinking days. Then avid followers of Dionysus, we cling now to more structured ways—they to the twelve steps, I to academia, still others to variations of the Ten Commandments.

In our younger days we clung to nothing, submitted to little—not time, not place, not oppressive codes of behavior, not rules save the wholly necessary. Unable to match our lives to the available community, we instead found freedom at its fringe, creating a Dionysian enclave that revolved around Joe's Bar.

"I'm-Rick-I'm-an-alcoholic—Hello-Rick—" The dialogue drones on, beaten and submissive. I hear tales illustrating the wrongness of wasted lives and the path we all once shared—it must be bad form to express how much fun was had. "Recovering" like the others, I too know addiction's pitfalls, but am not so removed from my experience that I cannot recall its pleasures. Unconvinced by the stories being told, I presume the tellers to be in denial.

Troubled as our lives may be by a past immersed in compulsion, there was something that drew us to the addictive lifestyle with overwhelming force. We loved drinking beer and smoking dope and the moments of sharing that we will never reconstitute outside the drunken arena. Ignoring that euphoria and focussing on the following hangover only recreates the dualism which pushed us toward excess. If we are to learn from our mistakes, must we not first remember them?

**

Driving through Pingree one sees a typical small farm town: a row of steel granaries, each holding fifty thousand bushels of grain; a few decrepit homes with unkempt yards; a grocery store with gas pumps; a school, its playground and baseball field. But my eyes draw toward two, more prominent buildings, each catering to its version of the sacred: Joe's Bar, situated in the townsite's center, and down the road a quarter mile the bankish looking Mormon Church.

As capitalists we know the Protestant ethic, of which Mormonism is just a quirky variety—the way to heaven, through one's works, comes from thrift, diligence, timeliness and the negation of base impulses. But we are less acquainted with—and even fearful of—the sacred path Joe's represents.

That path, still considered evil by many and unfortunate by most, was worshipped prior to Christianity as Pan, Bacchus and Dionysus. But one era's Gods become the next era's devils, and passing beyond Christianity those old gods-cum-devils become diseases, secularized by the medical community as sicknesses which can't be helped by the sufferer's actions. Our scientific studies pinpoint genetic causes for overimbibing, giving us excuse for our excesses.

But just as every plea to God is a cry to leave oneself, so is every call for another round. No more disease than excessive prayer, alcoholism is instead a quick, if redundant, route to God. A drinker senses his way as genuinely as the genuflector and his aim is with equal frequency untrue.

Joe's and the Pingree Church rise to approximately the same height, the abandoned depot's roof peak matching the church's steeple. The buildings sit on lots of relatively equal size, but the churchyard is paved and manicured, the tavern's lot dirt, gravel and weeds. The church, with an exterior built in the 1960's of brick and wood, still appears new compared to the eighty year old tavern's peeling paint, its sprawling shingles, its broken and slivered steps. We discern from appearance the two distinct voices, one a stern cry for order, the other a slack whisper of chaos. It is an old dichotomy, Apollonian structure versus Dionysian pleasure, which Pingree re-enacted with extra vigor.

**

Even in old Joe's hands the bar never prospered. A few Jack-Mormons, some immigrant Italians and a few stray gentiles barely kept the tavern running and his family fed. But after Joe died, subsequent managers had still less success, until the bar sat vacant through the middle seventies. In an area steeped in teetotaling Mormonism, few would expect anything else.

But the Dionysian sixties rocking America's foundations reached inland Idaho almost a decade later. On Christmas 1978, Joe's daughter appeared at the bar in her beat up fifty-one Dodge, ready to prepare the tavern for her turn at the helm.

Little did she know that she was the impetus for the eruption of an autocatalytic system, a self-generating entity which grows exponentially from its own positive feedback. Such systems arise from activators, a metaphoric analogue being basins to which rivers flow. Activators like a pebble on a plain, a rut on a prairie, or a pinprick in an egg cell can unsettle a stable universe and start the process which creates dunes, rivers and frogs. Ida—doe-eyed, five feet tall, hair straight to the waist—was such an activator, an unexpected and unimaginable clientele building around her catalyzing influence.

Within two months of her appearance—and before she had either a beer license or an operating permit from the Health Department—hippies, Vietnam vets, farmers' sons, carpenters and ironworkers had adopted the bar as their home. Then came professionals—lawyers and judges and engineers, the nearby town's newspaper editor. Bikers and Indians and hunters and college students, parachutists and old men, girls looking for guys, guys looking for girls—every outcast, black sheep and Jack-Mormon in the county came. Within two years the annual May blowout required forty-five kegs of beer.

Leaving the Bucket

**

Those who study *complexity* know there's a fine line between order and chaos. Adding a grain of sand to a pile in criticality can cause the entire system to collapse. Joe's' diverse crowd somehow maintained order without descending into chaos, but how, without enforcement, did it do so?

The work of Craig Reynolds may give a clue. Interested in the group behaviors of birds, fish and sheep and why their movements for the most part avoided chaos, he designed a computer program to simulate flocking, herding and schooling. Creating a large collection of computer images—he called them *boids*—, he placed them into an onscreen environment full of walls and other obstacles to see how they would interact. To keep the program simple, he gave each *boid* just three rules: 1) try to maintain a minimum distance from other objects in the environment, including other *boids*; 2) try to match velocities with nearby *boids*; 3) try to move toward the perceived center of mass of nearby *boids*. To his surprise, "flocks" spontaneously generated *every time* the program was run, no matter where he placed the *boids*.

We might infer from the experiment that just a few general, internal rules can generate order. We have all experienced the experiment's opposite, a large set of specific rules imposed from outside, often generating chaos in the form of informational overload and red-tape.

Ida's unspoken rules at Joe's were simple as those of the *boids*': tolerate others and be tolerable. This live and let live attitude, in combination with an infectiously likeable personality, received uncommon respect from the clientele—violence, normal in other area taverns, was absent.

**

The AA members file outside to smoke, to get some air fresher than the oppressive atmosphere of the meeting. Most have been coerced to attend by the legal system as part of their sentence for drunk driving or other alcohol or drug related offenses, but some are here willingly, either intensely remorseful about a recent binge or committed to the organization and their own successful recovery—which is always in process and never complete.

AA literature reminds the recovering that remission to addiction is always near, with chaos looming at every decision. The addict must be watchful and maintain the order of his life. This is difficult, for we Americans are obsessed with wildness, not order. We worship capitalist values based on structured living, but simultaneously wish to escape them—our history is laced with the urge to flee: colonists from British tyranny, Mormons from Eastern oppression, Wacoites and Rajneeshis from the overly ruled world-at-large. Our geographical frontiers exhausted, we moderns can only flee rule internally—and do so, through prayer or drugs.

Joe's, standing secretive beyond the tracks paralleling the highway, faces me through my schooldays in the playground a hundred yards distant.

Leaving the Bucket

Its religious competitor etches itself in my mind, as well, my friends dropping references to it at play, its relief society women, tithing collectors and "ward teachers" stopping regularly at our home to loosely tether my family to possible conversion—who knows, at any moment we might change our minds and join the fold.

On the first Sunday of every month, two adolescents come the six miles to our house to collect fast offerings, and Licorice, our black Labrador, chases them away if allowed—disliking either their suits or a virulent dogma. Occasionally missionaries stop, once threatening my father for not allowing them to baptize my sister. When she turned eighteen, he said, throwing them out, she would be able to decide for herself.

More coercive and covert influences followed. Primary and Mutual Night and Sunday School and Firesides, and a Seminary Building adjoining the junior and high schools and overshadowing all activities. Pioneer Days in July, and sports teams to lure me into the fold. All threats of order, as omnipresent as chaos is to the recovering AA member.

I learned yet more of Mormonism from osmosis: the Word of Wisdom, revelations, temple weddings, baptism for the dead, missions, tithing, the wearing of garments, an eternity with one's family—though no church member, the ubiquitous Mormon call still reached me.

But raised in the sixties I heard Dionysus' voice, and listened closely to his minimalist structures. That war was wrong seemed self-evident. That the religious who had taught me so refused to admit it required my active censure—I consciously turned from Apollo, opened myself to Dionysus.

No doubt few of Joe's drinkers pursued Dionysus as intentionally as I did, but conscious or not, all either evaded a life or searched for another. We all wanted "out"—whacked out, fucked up, plowed under, wired up—just as the Christian believer wishes freedom from the world.

What made some of us alcoholics and others "in control" mimicked the difference between religion and magic. Both the alcoholic and the worshipper of magic enact ritual to influence the gods, while the truly religious do so only to approach them. Selfishness characterizes the magician, selflessness the religious. Every addict is a magician, re-imbibing his sacred ritual of choice. Shopping, prayer, heroin or alcohol: having found the quickest path from himself to the sacred, he re-enacts the ritual to return.

But when God turns his back on this inauthentic act, the addict turns up his ritual worship. His habits worsen as failures gather, until God is lost in churning and vacant ritual.

**

People flee from anarchy as well as order—it seems we want neither freedom nor enslavement. Those crushed by overly structured religion flee to Dionysus, those addicted to chaos rush to Apollo. Moderation, then, must be the key, in measures of which I'm unsure.

Leaving the Bucket

While moderation might be natural, nature is not moderate. Up the road from my home Russian olive trees overwhelm a subwater wasteland, choking out all competitors. Neighboring farmers curse the weedy tree, as only a constant cultivation allays its spread. So thick in some places that a deer might not be able to walk through, the olive trees send up suckers, spreading outward as well as up, their thorny branches drawing blood from any who challenge their domain.

Their gray-green leaves shine silvery when turned by the wind, and in early summer their plentiful blossoms send a honeyed, memorable scent—and allergies—for miles. The equally hated magpies build large, sloppy nests in their protective branches, and other birds eat the Russian olive seeds and expel them randomly elsewhere, expanding the tree's range. It is a Dionysian tree, beautiful and wholly unruly.

In some of the world's more elaborate gardens, plantsmen utilize a technique called *pleaching* to create artificial structures, most often arched, tunnel-like canopies of shrubs or trees. The practice entails tying and sometimes grafting the branches of young trees together, so that as they grow they intertwine as one. Thus, saplings along one side of a path can be joined to those on the other. After the trees grow together for an appropriate time the gardener loosens his ties, and the branches spring up to form an arch somewhat higher and tighter than when bound.

The unruly Russian olive may have never been pleached, and its metaphorical opposite, the palm, which grows skyward without widening or sending out branches, is likely a poor candidate for the technique, as well. Its path is straight and narrow, its fruit, like heaven's, are at the peak of its reach, and it ceases growing only when the wind topples it.

But, unable to dwell solely with either Dionysus or Apollo, the addict must pleach similarly unlike companions. One needs heavy pruning, the other a constant restraint—this much order, this much chaos, each strains against the other. In winter, the leaves fallen, sun filters through the pleached limbs, and in summer the branches shade those underneath. Only windbreaks by themselves, together Joe's Bar and Alcoholics Anonymous form a sort of odd shelter, sublimely, if not beautifully, intertwined.

"I'm Dave, I'm an alcoholic—" "Hi Dave—" I mumble along, trying to not belong without offending the others.

SALTUS—LEAVING THE BUCKET

I'm meeting two former girlfriends at Luke's Island, another rural tavern just six miles from Joe's, in which I was once accused of holding stock. Arriving, I recognize a regular from my drinking days sitting with them at the bar, attempting with his cowboy wit and charm to seduce them. To his chagrin, they slide down the bar to greet me. He protests to no avail, and seeing he has lost all opportunity of capturing coup, challenges loudly, "That Ralph, now he's gone to college, he's so smart he's stupid."

I shrug. There's a tale about two men fishing for crayfish—one Indian, one white—which illuminates the meaning of his statement. Having filled their buckets with their catch, they go off for a drink together to celebrate their success. When they return, the white man's crayfish have escaped while the Indian's bucket is still full. The Indian explains to the perplexed white, "I only caught Indian crayfish." When the white remains confused, the Indian explains further. "When an Indian crayfish tries to get out of the bucket, the others grab him and keep him in."

When someone in a relationship instigates change, either the other member or the relationship itself must change, too, in order for it to survive. Ethnic groups and religions work hard to prevent members from changing or leaving—guilt, shame and coercion being among their tools—but smaller entities like families and social groups also exert pressure on members to stay the same so they can keep their character intact. Though Randy's words may be ill-chosen, I understand his meaning: I have changed, we now communicate on different levels, and he wishes to drag me back into the bucket.

**

My first time out of the bucket of rural alcoholism lasted one semester at a local university. Unable to make any sort of lasting ties, I moved back, tail between legs, to a fate of farmwork and drinking. A year later I summoned the will to try again, thinking this time that by commuting I would at least evade the loneliness of the city full of strangers. But one morning, a month into the semester and in the grip of some small despair, I stopped partway to school and turned back, ending another attempt at freedom with a small act of useless—but seemingly necessary at the time—defiance.

I tried again the next year, made it a year and a half before suffering a breaking angst, slipped back for a bit, and then at last finished out a degree. Again I moved back to the country—a bachelor's degree in American Studies holds little value in the American workplace—and fell into old ways for a short time. Only with the aid of love was I able to finally leave, to finally change.

Leaving the Bucket

Most change can be viewed as a creative process of development, a process described by Richard Rabkin as having five stages: preparation, "thrustration," incubation, transformation and consolidation.

According to Rabkin, when in the preparation stage, we examine our material—our possibilities—in a near-random manner. In the *thrustration* stage which follows, the period of labor pains, we exhaust possible solutions to the problems we encounter in that material, often becoming blocked. After putting our work aside and "sleeping on it" (the incubation period) a sudden change and transformation (what Rabkin calls *saltus*) occurs, a sort of enlightenment at having seen a new pattern or solving a problem.

During the last and perhaps most important phase, consolidation, the individual assimilates the new learning, making it a part of his being. Some mentally deficient individuals, often able to make the *saltus* or leap in understanding, cannot, however, maintain it. Though again and again they make the developmental leap, they never stay on the other side.

An alcoholic mimics that failure. He may become sober for long periods of time again and again, but slip back into drunkenness each time. Unable to consolidate sobriety he remains "deficient" in his creative process.

**

Americans have long detested the intellectual. Our recognized philosophy, pragmatism, associates truth with *what works* rather than *what is*. In rural and blue-collar areas, commonsense rules, and the myths founding self-understanding often include stories of dumb engineers and professional in-laws who cannot so much as carry on a normal conversation. Having had their lives adjudged negatively by experts and their tastes belittled by critics, they in turn poke fun at white-collar workers and academics for their pumped up airs and lack of worldly ability.

A model student in my youth with promise of a great future, I sided with the intellectual experts. In their analysis of backwoods America, they often correctly unraveled the backwardness of the less-educated and often bigoted. But pointing out another's problems is no great feat, and when I found myself in the position of farm laborer I discovered how little I knew, though by academic standards I might be a genius.

Now, I sympathize with Randy and his ilk—pragmatic knowledge founds our existence, giving us time for the luxury of more refined analysis and thought. I can only absorb his barbs—he no doubt can tie more kinds of knots than me, is a better mechanic, can weld, can wire his home for electricity, and he would not ascribe any worth to my claims of knowledge. Forced to choose only one sort of understanding, I would take his, the more fundamental.

Thankfully, I am not limited by that choice.

**

Randy's still married, but most of the old drinking crowd is divorced now. Many split up, having lived together "in sin" happily for years, only after they

Leaving the Bucket

married. That single word, "married," transformed their freely undertaken relationship into one which was legally bound, creating resentment where none existed prior.

But some of the wives just sought change, either through education or a corporate job, having found their lives unfulfilling once they'd wholly adopted the cloak of marriage. Weekends at the local bar, rowdy parties until dawn in homes they were trying to fashion as semi-sacred, lost the luster seen earlier in their lives.

Even many who didn't chase around the bars have ended up separated, their wives tired too of the rural homelife they signed up for. Some of these *wanted* a more vibrant life, began hitting the bars when they hadn't before, but most felt left behind by the wave of working women they deemed as their peers. The rural community where wives once interacted and shared work and interests disappeared when they gained access to automobiles—the grass is always greener on the other side, and that is just where they headed.

The men consequently fear change—often, rightly so. When wives indicate they want to go to college, it means to husbands far more than that. The women play down, even ridicule, those fears, but for once the masculine half of the relationship is the more intuitive.

Education *is* a leap outside the realm of their prior relationships. It entails meeting new people, encountering new ideas, and a new way of interacting. One cannot learn or experience anything without it in some way affecting other behaviors, and compared with the busy academic and urban life a rural existence seems paltry. The wives, unaware of this fact, allay no fears with their ignorance.

"'Til death do us part; through richer or poorer"—these commitments mean little now, when if-then clauses come implicit in every agreement. If I need to "grow" or "find myself"—or have any acceptable reason—I am relieved of my responsibility and allowed to break any commitment. Though not every relationship should remain intact, no real relationship can stand against the qualities of one imagined, and those leaving old commitments cannot fully understand the meaning of new ones as they understand the old. If we seek a way out of a relationship, perhaps we indeed should leave it, but if we seek escape from an imperfect commitment because it pales aside one imagined as better we should remain—we cannot avoid imperfect being, not in a present nor imagined world.

Implicit rules govern any relationship, and can only be changed by agreement—if the context of a marriage becomes too stifling, the stifled needs to express the needed change. But if we believe our desires for difference or change as a "right", we exclude our spouses from discussion, and the relationship devolves from shared status to one of opposing wills.

Relationships which survive change have either excessive luck or meta-rules, rules which govern the way the members change their lesser rules. In relationships of power, between those considering themselves separate individuals and thus in conflict, no such meta-rules exist, but where partners submit to an overarching agreement a leap into consolidated understanding can occur.

The farmer's wife seeks a way out of a too static or sacred homelife and heads to the bar, the drunk's wife seeks a way out of a too wild life and heads to structure—religion, education, employment. We seek difference and change, demand structure and security, and no relationship can wholly encompass both unlimited desires.

**

At my older sisters' request, I pester my parents to go to the drive-in, where the blockbuster "Cleopatra" plays. As dairy farmers tied to the twice daily milking of cows, we never have time to do such things, but for some reason my parents concede.

At the drive-in I am bemused by my sisters' strong interest, for all I can see is blurred color on a big screen. Asked afterward how I liked the movie, I reveal my lack of vision—what I experienced as a normal world I would, after acquiring glasses, discover was severely lacking.

Randy's screen is no doubt blurred in some way, just as mine was. He may be as unconscious of his blindness as I was of mine. Ours are two versions of Plato's cave, our backs to the wall as we watch shadows we think are real, but are instead just the removed images of originals. But if we allow for other visions, other versions of reality, we lose the comfort of the sight we know, even though in doing so we may gain a wider vista. And even if we want to change, to gain our way into a new place and a new way of seeing, we rarely have the tools to bridge our ways to new worlds and contexts—inevitably, the tools come afterwards, with those worlds. But at any given time we do have two techniques available to us—an admission of ignorance and a flush of tolerance. Making our world safe by hardening our beliefs and prejudices, we prevent ourselves from entering new worlds, but by acknowledging ignorance we open the borders to those worlds, through tolerance we allow others in and simultaneously ourselves out.

But if we all were wholly tolerant, borders would break down. Ethnicities would be lost, detail would lose meaning. As we imagine ourselves climbing the ladder of enlightenment, let us praise the intolerant we believe to be below us. They are the possessors of potential change, the keepers of societal structure—without stasis, there is no change.

**

Wittgenstein writes: "Let us suppose that a game is such that whoever begins can always win by a particular simple trick. But this has not been realized;--so it is a game. Now someone draws our attention to it;--and it stops being a game...

"That means...the other man did not draw our attention to anything; he taught us a different game in place of our own.—But how can the new game have made the old one obsolete?—We now see something different, and can no longer naively go on playing."

Leaving the Bucket

Each time I returned to alcoholism, I felt more and more divorced from the game of drunkenness. Though I went through the motions, I lacked the mental involvement to experience debauchery authentically—I didn't want to play anymore. Having learned the unconscious rules of the alcoholic's world, I was thrust into a new game with a new vision.

Almost a decade out of the bucket, I am still learning how to play the new game.

Randy is still at the bar.

READING THE GRAIN

As a pre-adolescent I played Scrabble with intensity, keeping records of win-loss percentages, highest scores, largest number of points won by and a host of other trivial statistics. Over a period of some years and thousands of games, I became able to discern the differences between the woodgrain on the backs of the tiles. The "J" and the "Q" and the "X" and the "Z"—big scoring letters—stood out vividly, as did the blanks, and it's likely I can still separate them from the other tiles in the game that still roosts in my parents' closet.

The knowledge presented me with the opportunity to cheat, but not wanting to, it provided a different dilemma: if I deliberately chose the letter I sought I would be cheating my opponent, but if I intentionally did not choose it I would be cheating myself. How does one, then, reintroduce what is random at one level when the pattern which organizes it at another has been discovered?

I closed my eyes and mixed up the letters. This randomized my draw somewhat, but my fingers still remembered their general location. Only with my brother's aid in mixing up the letters—and my choosing not to look—could I reintroduce a semblance of the unknown, make fair again what knowledge had made unfair.

Leaving the Bucket

**

Only through "noise" can new patterns be achieved. We need chaos from which to create more elaborate order, but also to erase old patterns. Some years beyond Scrabble as entertainment, I go to Joe's to do both.

According to Gregory Bateson, an alcoholic's style or pattern of sobriety drives him to drinking as a "corrective measure." The bar life can be either a needed chaos in an overly ordered sobriety, or a necessary order for the overly chaotic life. It is, in each instance, new information, a "difference that makes a difference," in Batesonian terminology.

Loud music, raucous laughter, the multiple smells of tobacco, beer and sometimes (if Ida isn't looking) marijuana; foosballs banging into goals, pool balls clacking against one another, slurred declarations of lifelong loyalty; conversations between two, between three, between more; banter, glasses clinking, and vulgar repertoire; antiques on the wall, a new draught beer, a chili Ida rushed together: chaos to break my summer's ordered life of ninety hour work weeks, chaos to disturb my winter's ordered life of no work at all.

And when my life is too chaotic, when I can only think of how I should go-to-school-straighten-up-get-a-girl-find-a-real-job, I can stop by earlier in the day, when just Ida and Uncle Johnny sit on opposite sides of the bar relating dull stories related before. The heater fan blows incessantly. The early sun stares through the east windows. The mirror and glass reflect only surface. I sip at the beer and quietude, my life's movements suddenly more manageable.

I do not read the backs of tiles here. Learning the game of alcoholism, I am inside its rules, not out. I am interested in how so many different types of people can fit together when elsewhere they do not; interested in how I can get as wild as I please yet not be snubbed. With my attention on experiencing the seemingly random, I can turn away from the rules that lurk in the background.

**

I try to forget the grain patterns as I select my letters, instead I remember them more vividly. "We are condemned to remember what we contrive to forget," writes Douglas Flemons, who as a therapist deals with such paradox. Patients ask him to accomplish the impossible task of excising a part of them they wish wasn't there—i.e., the spouse who cannot but wants to forget the other's infidelity. But as they try to forget they can only remember: as the transgression is the impetus for the act of forgetting, it must paradoxically be present to be erased.

We cannot actively forget, then, but drugs can temporarily take our attention away from remembering, give the impression our memories are gone. Flemons analogizes bad memories with an image in bas-relief, which, when sanded, disappears. In this way, drugs can sand a life down to the level of surrounding stimuli, making unpleasant memories less the foreground of attention.

For a hundred binges drinking buoys my hopes briefly, makes me think I can leap from my "style of sobriety." But increasingly, on mornings after, they sink, as I've returned to what I sought to escape: I still wake alone, am still without meaningful work or friend. Though I continue to drink, hoping against hope, I know I try to cheat chance: drunkenness will solve no problems, in the morning I will sober.

I know what's on the tile's other face. I have broken the rules of chance governing the game of addiction, taken the veil away that allows me to believe the period of inebriation is real, and have instead made those hours an imaginary subset of life. Losing the random joy that is alcohol's gift, I gain predictability, its curse.

**

In the 1980's, two college basketball coaches—Dean Smith of North Carolina and John Thompson of Georgetown—perfected a stalling technique called the "four corner offense." When their teams gained suitable leads they placed a player in each corner of the front court and played what was essentially "keep-away." When opposing players rushed toward the ball, the man in possession passed to an open man in another corner. After minutes of failing to take the ball away, the defense would try harder and harder and finally overcommit themselves, allowing easy baskets that extended the stalling team's lead.

Technically within the game's rules since there was no shot clock to force offenses to shoot, the method ran counter to the unwritten spirit of basketball. Winning replaced playing as the game's desired end, manipulating rules rather than expressing skills became the nature of the game. Rules, as the unconscious foundations that facilitate any form of play or relationship, must be kept in the background, not the fore.

Smith and Thompson had read the backs of the tiles, broken the unspoken agreement not to use their extra knowledge. After their ploy continued for several years and threatened the game's integrity and players' and fans' interest, a forty-five second shot clock was introduced to end the practice.

The game has since changed dramatically.

**

Ida falls in love approximately every six months. Since I've started drinking here there's been two musicians, a carpenter, a well-driller, and a reporter. There were others before, there will be others after, but following each affair she has no period of cynicism, just a blank slate on which to renew gullibility. She is like the young child wishing to hear the same joke again and again, laughing as much the last as the first time it's told.

I have loved only twice: loved love itself once, a real woman another time—and already I am wary of another try. I envy, while simultaneously disdaining, her.

Leaving the Bucket

In his works, Bateson regularly cites a seminal study of learning performed with dolphins. In the study, a dolphin was rewarded with food once it performed a particular behavior, then reinforced when it repeated the act. After repeated rewards for having learned the behavior, the trainer discontinued the reward, upsetting the dolphin. During further interaction, the dolphin was then rewarded when it showed a different, untrained behavior—say, a flip of the tail—and the trainer repeated the sequence of reinforcement.

After several cycles of rewarding new behaviors, then discontinuing the rewards, the dolphin one day came to the pool very excited. Once the trainer came into view it exhibited several new behaviors, some never seen before in dolphins. The dolphin had "learned to learn", according to Bateson, had learned that the researcher was after not a *particular* behavior but a *class* of behaviors—"new" ones.

Ida knows when an individual man or relationship goes bad, but doesn't know the class of men and relationships or why they deteriorate. Within a narrow framework she can repeat what she knows, but she doesn't learn from that knowledge to expand it into a class of higher order learning.

She is lucky. I would give greatly to be as easily entertained by the thousandth drunk and I had by the first.

**

After my brother knew I could pick an important letter at will, he viewed me with distrust and frequently accused me of cheating. I responded with indignity, thinking my act of honesty had undeservedly inspired distrust. But my admission, unbeknownst to me, *required and tested* trust, rather than building it.

Some knowledge is best kept arcane. Once a level in logical type has been leaped and a relationship breached, it requires too much work to repair—a new "world" must be built. Having the power to breach the rules of chance and randomness which governed Scrabble, I had to be trusted to never use it. I forced my opponents to depend on my trustworthiness, rather than inspiring them to trust me.

Georgetown and North Carolina played as well with a shot clock as without, but basketball changed as a result of their coaches' actions. I shared information with my brother, showing him the letters I knew, and afterward mistrusted him as he did me. Since Joe's has closed, Ida's serial partners have gained a longer shelf life, so she too has learned upon repeated effort.

I have quit drinking heavily—or as T. S. Eliot would say, it quit me—because both its bas-relief excitement wore away and the background behind it raised. I grew more and more to know how the game would end, making it more tedious, though I would for years return to it, still hopeful. I later took interest in other, academic "games," the rules of which would also be unveiled. I gained a family, as well, taking attention from my self-pity and the habit I once cultivated.

But the process continues: if we play a game enough, we eventually learn to discern what lies behind it and its tools. We can choose to cheat, we can cultivate ignorance as long as possible, or we can withhold our powers once we learn to learn. Unsure of which path is best, I choose not to choose, refrain for at least the present from reading the grain.

HUMOR AND EXILE: A RETURN TO DUTY

During World War II, my mother worked for the Nazi leader Fritz Saukel, who was in charge of "foreign labor" at Buchenwald, a concentration camp near Weimar. He would eventually be found guilty of war crimes and sentenced to death at the Nuremburg trials. When the American general marching on Weimar called him to demand the city's surrender, Saukel began the flight away, calling Hitler from the village of Frauendorf. My mother overheard part of the conversation—Hitler telling Saukel to keep going, that there was yet something to save.

But knowing the gig was up, Saukel sent the office pool to safety in a small village in East Germany. Three of the girls, including my mother, quartered with a doctor and his wife who, fearful of the enemy's taste for rape, had sent their own daughters to the mountains,.

For three weeks the girls lived on gathered nettles and a bit of sausage for which they had traded the office typewriter. My mother intended to walk home to her family near the Czechoslovakian border, until she discovered the Americans had already passed them by and taken over that area. With nowhere else to go, in the latter half of May and the war over, she rode

Leaving the Bucket

back to Weimar with the city's police who had also sought refuge in the same village. So eager were they to return to Weimar that they left the remainder of their invaluable black market sausage in the village.

My mother immediately took work with the Americans, who had taken over Buchenwald, transcribing prisoner testimony which would later be used at Nuremburg. On July first, when the border between the Germanies became official, an offer by messenger came—if she wanted to move to the American camp being moved to Wiesbaden, she should be at the camp at five o'clock with her belongings. She accepted the offer, along with the lone suitcase which comprised her personal property.

Saukel, in hiding, gave himself up some weeks later.

Sometimes we seek chaos, preferring it to an overweening order. Safe in a country village, my mother sought promise in a war-torn city; hidden in the wilds of Germany, Saukel chose certain imprisonment. Either duty or familiarity calls, both of them desires for lost patterns.

**

I haven't drunk a drop in eight days. I read, go for long walks out in the rocky sagebrush or down along the reservoir flats—anything to avoid Joe's, my drinking haven. All day I wait for sleep, hoping to keep my night unconscious and long, just that many more hours away from inebriation.

The mornings are all promise. I wake to pheasants booming, the birds insisting first sunlight. I hear Pat, the fish hatchery foreman, drive by on his way to the lower pond. There will be only occasional traffic until afternoon, when he returns on his way back from the hatchery.

I breakfast methodically, lengthening out this task as I do all others, then walk the one and seven tenths miles to the post office. The dew just burning off, I saunter over gravel and dust, pass by the Russian olives which infest the neighbor's acreage. I hope, stretch the hope, that a letter will come which will give the promise to keep me sober the rest of the day.

By Ruff's artesian well, through the crossroads, by the swamp and the stream which feeds the Tube—the local swimming hole--, over the railroad tracks, onto the pavement and into the townsite. I unlock my box at the post office, smell a scented envelope. My heart uplifts as I see calligraphy painstakingly written. I walk the one point seven miles back, savoring a hope that has the taste of love and freedom.

**

During the latter part of World War II, Southeast Idaho farmers, their sons gone to battle, needed laborers to harvest their vast potato acreages. Any available body was commandeered, including a crew from Jamaica in "natty dress", whites transported in from the South and thousands of Japanese-Americans who had been incarcerated as a threat to the American government.

Leaving the Bucket

The farmers also utilized a number of Italian and German prisoners of war. The government erected several temporary camps from which farmers could draw their workers. Under Geneva convention rules, farmers could only work the prisoners a set amount—far less than the hundred sacks common to a local picker—for which they must pay them a fair wage.

A local farmer tells of witnessing a guard handing his rifle to a prisoner as he crossed a fence, and the prisoner handing the rifle back once he'd crossed. Though regulations prohibited farmers and their families from interacting with the prisoners, some wives baked bread for their captive workers. The wartime atmosphere—in these cases, at least—might seem less stressful than that which the prisoners had left.

But on at least one occasion prisoners still attempted escape. A pair of Italians slipped out of camp, inspiring fear in the local populace, but were easily found the next morning meandering along a busy road, heading back to camp. Their only complaint, according to the local paper, was of the cold area temperatures.

No matter how uncomfortable or imprisoning a context, we may still, like those Italian prisoners, long to return to it, once having measured it against the alternatives.

**

My mother last saw Saukel in Wiesbaden, recognizing him as captive in the back of an American

Forces car as she walked by with the American major for whom she worked. The major noticed her distress, asked its source, and after she explained her shock he directed her to go back and speak with her former boss.

But when she tapped on the car's window to apologize for working for his captors, Saukel just put his fingers to his lips, indicating silence. She left, never speaking with him again. Fifty years later she still expresses guilt for having switched sides, though she justifies her actions as a product of the chaos following war.

**

I read the letter slowly, every word a balm for my wounded soul. Though we converse through only this narrow window of words on paper, the light she throws both warms and illuminates.

I read it again, place it reverently with the dozens of others letters she has sent, for an hour steep in its wake. When emotion subsides, I write her a missive, hoping to cast equal warmth upon her.

She is married, it is true, but wrongly so. Her imprisonment seems, from her words, as dark and oppressive as my own unlimited freedom. Fellow captives, fellow saviors, planning escapes, planning rescues, this single entwined mass of promise we each experience at a distance as a single, shared entity, a living thing.

The letter finished, to be sent the next day, I pick up a novel by Hermann Hesse. In a few hours I'll have devoured it and started another, having nothing to disturb the author's lyrical intent. In between books, I listen to current ballads and write poetry that will one day make me shudder with embarrassment. I anticipate receiving tomorrow's letter, bask in that emotion until it leaves, then write her again.

I have a phone but cannot risk calling, but when desperate she will call me, so I hover close, change just that near, a movement from aloneness to holy sharing.

**

America was promise.
My father was American.
My mother married promise.

A contorted syllogism similar to this must have run through my mother's mind in 1948. After two years in post-war Germany, single with a young son, things were not easy. And having a sense of guilt for working for the Americans after once rising so high serving the Party, she must have felt exiled by her own people, thus wanted out, was ready for escape. My father was a way out of her context.

Anyone would have sufficed, I suspect. Perhaps any marriage begins this way, a ripe moment giving meeting to mutual prey. Nearly thirty, having served seven years in the military, my father needed my mother as a way out of his context. When need grows sufficiently great, love arises in those who believe in it, purpose in those who do not.

Ralph Thurston

**

Gregory Bateson listed humor—along with such diverse practices as art, schizophrenia, ritual and violence—as a *transcontextual* behavior. These are ways of transcending worlds too imprisoning, ways which can shatter one's current level of existence. But art can be either dogmatic or uplifting, can either reify or transcend reality. And violence and schizophrenia, even when effective, may simply make old patterns more virile (and virulent).

Humor, like other transcontextual tools, can either stultify its practitioners or propel them to new understandings. Laughing, we may either escape an overly routinized life or further deepen a problematic belief. Some humor, such as satire and parody, depends on another's work for its sustenance. Parasitical, it primarily destroys, while simultaneously strengthening its own practitioners' borders.

But there are more complex humors that straddle multiple meanings, instruct listeners in contradiction and paradox. Here, a punchline often synthesizes misunderstandings, shattering them not only with laughter but a new vision and comprehension of the world.

But just as a prisoner may venture out, then sheepishly return, and just as one given freedom may instead choose certain imprisonment, a joker and his audience may each turn to a stale present in which they laugh emptily, and away from rich transcendence which, separating them from a comfortable and unthinking past, can easily but wrongly be seen as exile.

"Knock, knock," says my four year old daughter, some fifteen years later.

"Who's there?" I ask.

"Orange."

"Orange who?"

"Orange Mr."

She laughs heartily, and I laugh at her laugh, with no idea what she finds hilarious. When she quiets, we repeat the joke, and she jiggles with mirth again.

Perhaps it is Zen humor, a height of awareness which I will never reach.

Old contexts wither and shrink, become old jokes, their punchlines worn out like my daughter's. We can forget an old pattern's redundancy—a difficult task—or convince ourselves it is a new one—for some, just as difficult—or somehow create or elevate into a new context. But this we can do only without conscious purpose.

**

For my mother, the long trip from highrolling Nazi Germany to Springfield, Idaho, must have been a Dante-esque descent through the gradations of Hell. In severe distress, we imagine futures which exceed reality by the exact amount which our present falls insufficient to our needs. The wonderful America she incessantly heard about from the many GI's missing it no doubt structured the promising futures which ran through her mind. Home, wherever it is, always sounds like the last, best place—the GIs' recollections of theirs may not have been wholly accurate.

Flying across the Atlantic, she and her son undoubtedly suffered the discomfort of air travel as one engine burned out and smoke filled the cabin, and the train ride across the open plains must have given her anxious intimations. But as she left Salt Lake City and witnessed the wide open deserts with towns becoming smaller and more and more infrequent, her heart must have shattered into innumerable jagged shards, along with all the promises she had conjured. When she reached Springfield and the two bedroom wooden shack where my father, she and her son would live along with her husband's parents, she may have been mistaken for a corpse.

It would get worse.

The winter of 1948-9 is still the most severe on Idaho record. Drifts rose above telephone lines, railroads and highways were shut down and the temperatures plummeted as the winds grew stronger. My parents spoke of ice on the blankets in the morning, where their breaths collected as what must have seemed her punishment for leaving home.

She would have left, she has said many times, had she been able. But my grandmother, a humorless Mormon matriarch, censored her mail and kept that avenue of rescue closed, perhaps rightfully doubting her loyalty. Penniless and already pregnant, with her alternatives nil and her resources minimal, she had to stay where she was, unable to contact outside help.

Without even a warm bed or fresh water, isolated in a rural homestead with a hateful mother-in-law,

Leaving the Bucket

only a survivor—one with hope—could endure. I assume that hope was escape.

**

For two months, the window between us widens. She calls collect almost daily, we speak for at least an hour. Once a week, twice a week she visits, our love swelling my days like buds ripening to flower. I no longer fear the bar, having an alternative, no longer drink until drunkenness. Propelled from a routinized alcoholism, I look forward to a future of promise.

The telephone operators know us by now, familiar enough with our voices as she places the calls which I accept. I imagine us as a storyline in their workplace, their kind voices encouragement for our future together.

She says she is preparing to leave her husband.

Promise nears reality, and fear solidifies. Now I must perform. All the issues which drove me toward drink now surface again to be challenged. But, having another chance to really live, I will not run.

Prisoners nearing parole often bolt at the last second, risking further incarceration but unable to stand the last few days of anticipation. And others choose to stay in prison, fearing the outside world where they have already failed to fit in. Of all this I am aware, am of consequence intent on having patience.

**

My mother, who wished to justify to Saukel what she believed to be her treachery, still rationalizes the Holocaust as a byproduct of war. It is a start—she never admitted the Holocaust as possible until she was well into her seventies, when she read a book from the local library having too much information to deny. How, she wondered, when she had gone to SS parties in Buchenwald, when she worked with those close to the events, when she lived but a couple miles away, could such things happen without her knowing?

The "witch of Buchenwald"—the camp commander's wife—was a nice woman, she tells me, and couldn't possibly have made lampshades of human skin and tables of human bone, as purported. Brought up on dozens of like tales, I see doubly: what people appear to be and what they are may differ, though I do not know yet which face one can deem as true.

**

In early August, the bad news: she "has to" give her husband one more chance, give him the rope he needs to hang himself.

We return, she to duty, a context of bad marriage, I to a limbo exiled from love, self-exiled from all prior habit.

**

War brides, for millennia a sort of coup for the victors of battle, live in a perverse form of exile. Having forsaken one community that may see them

Leaving the Bucket

as traitorous but not believed by their new group as sincere, they may spend their remaining life isolated from both those left and those whom they seek to join.

My mother may have only imagined herself a victim of persecution, but she felt so, nonetheless. When we as children brought home from school the stories of war crimes, when movies portrayed Nazis as evil or bumbling, when those who lost husbands or sons in the war met her gaze, she sensed the community's accusation.

Exiled—by self or community—for fifty years, she paid for her sins without ever having asked for forgiveness. Had she done so, she may have regained an innocence she'd never truly lost.

**

Without her letters or her company, I have only two contexts from which to choose, and I split my time between them. Home, I re-read her letters, try to be what I would be were I with her. Failing, I return to the bar, drink, get drunk, but my binges lack the depth they once had, no longer being accidental in nature. Conscious of his destructive pattern, an addict loses his habit's value without decreasing its considerable cost.

**

My mother returned to Germany after my father died, hoping to rekindle what she'd left nearly fifty years prior. She went through the list of people she wanted to see—old co-workers, boyfriends, family—but most had died. One, an SS, had left no traceable trail, though four months later, back in the U.S., she received word of his death—he no doubt had a past necessary to hide, even from her.

The old town she had lived in had changed completely, become unrecognizable. On one street near the border between the Germanies, the rubble from the war still remained. For fifty years she had harbored that rubble, a secret hope to return to salvation, but now that hope was gone, too. Her return to Idaho was a return to duty, a final trek into exile.

**

She came back. We married. I left the context of alcoholism, but only because it refused my return—not addiction, not love nor fascism, can be felt as strongly once seen as illusion. One cannot, Heraclitus wrote, step into the same river twice.

Hindus believe that Brahman hides himself from himself in this world in a playful game of illusion and belief. Losing oneself in either nation or another is like hiding oneself from oneself or laughing at one's own joke. It requires enlightenment, denial, or childlike ignorance, all of which still evade me.

The tools to him who can handle them.
--Thomas Carlyle

TOOLS (NO PUEDO)

I try to remember the irrigation system's components: the frog is the squat thing sitting on the valve, which screws into a triple legged piece called the spider. The telescope attaches the wheel line to the valve opener, and down the line rainbirds spray out water and sit above the drain dogs (bird-dogs, I assume), which—

I will never remember it all. There are ten thousand things: come-alongs and easy-outs and handyman jacks and keyways—but no Kierkegaard, Plato, Sartre or Lao-Tse. Working on a modern farm, apparently, is how I must learn humility.

Though I grew up on a farm, I am a generation behind. My father, more interested in fishing than agriculture, didn't share today's farmer's addiction to technology. Tools were for him as they are to Wendell Berry: if not cheaper or better, if they do not make one's life more independent than those they seek to replace they should not be accepted and used.

Our tricycle type tractor had half the power of the John Deeres my classmates bragged of having. Our sole truck, an unlicensed 1948 Studebaker, had suspect brakes, a metal arm that served as a turn signal, and a muffler that spewed exhaust into the cab. We wired together old, used equipment and bought others'

Ralph Thurston

discarded irrigation pipes, latching on to trends only as they left, so as to afford their usefulness rather than their prestige. I learned from my father, then, not a grasp of the future, but a sense of living in the present, within one's means.

He has provided me at best the tools of a peasantlike animal husbandry—I know my way around a dairy. I can use a pitchfork and stack hay, shovel grain, feed calves and herd cows, but I cannot weld or mechanic, the skills necessary in a modernized agribusiness. Though under strict tutelage I might make the leap from organic products to wood, this world of metal is far beyond my reach.

Chisels, cutting torches, wheel pullers, sprockets— a thousand tools and parts fill the farmer's shop, all items to recall and classify. Each is a mystery to me, so unskilled a handyman that my nickname to the Mexican harvest help is "*no puedo*," which I find out years later means "not able."

**

Man fashions tools, but those same tools shape him. As systems comprised of our tools, what we work on, and ourselves—what Gregory Bateson would call "mind"—we may not, hard as we try, extricate ourselves from our environment: if we work cement, we will in some way be cement, and will respond to the rest of the world as cement responds to us. Few competent woodworkers lack the patience and method which wood insists upon; steelworkers and engineers are known for thinking linearly as if direct and sufficient

Leaving the Bucket

force could solve all problems—which, in the world of metal, perhaps can; the true gardener has a sense of ecology, having learned through working with the earth the rhythms and relationships of organic life. Where we make our thrusts into the world determines what we withdraw from it, for every material has its constraints defining both its forms and our talents.

Drugs and alcohol are tools, shaping us as we use them. They can ease the way to sexual gratification, pry a "yes" from a previously reluctant partner. They can make camaraderie more likely, can be used temporarily to forget, dull or even excite. But like all tools and techniques, they can bewitch those using them, those forgetting why they were first put in hand. Being only one component of Batesonian mind, they can unbalance the obsessed user who separates them from their context. I am such a user.

My labor is a context of submissiveness and inferiority, where I lack the mechanical skills and strength of my co-workers. When equipment breaks or something needs lifted I am reminded of my inabilities and mock myself, even if my co-workers do not, for my dependency on others. In the winter, when there is no work, there are other reasons to feel small and useless: I am reminded of my lack of social skills, my inability to enter either academia or the corporate world, institutions distant from a rural life.

But in the world of the bar in Pingree, I need neither mechanical nor social ability, need manipulate nothing more than my wallet, a beer bottle, a stereo or a joint—and this I am competent to do. Thus, to the degree I lack confidence in the rest of my life, alcohol helps me gain pride at Joe's.

At work my jokes fall flat, my observations are met with bemusement. I have taken to leaving sentences unfinished, realizing no one listens. But under the spell of alcohol and in the presence of others who, like me, are a generation behind, I feel witty and bright as anyone. Drink gives me what I am missing, albeit in excessive amount: I often drink to unconsciousness, a measure of my humility at work.

**

Though I cannot perform the maintenance work of a modern farm, I can at least drive a tractor. Two thousand hours in a seven month period I sit, manipulating pedals, buttons and levers. Plow, disc, chisel, rip, drill, spray, combine, dig, swath, bale, stack—all through the miracle of machines.

In the spring I plow the stubble, then disc and harrow it down. Afterward, I pack the soil and plant hundreds of acres of wheat and barley. I rip and chisel the fields where potatoes will grow, disc and roller-harrow the clods under, then mark the rows.

Normally I do not worry about driving straight as other farm workers do. A plow turns the soil if driven crookedly or straight, and the grain combine cannot distinguish between the linear and the curved. But potato harvesters require straight and uniform rows or they will damage the tubers during harvest, so as much as I despise straight lines—"if they give you ruled paper, write the other way," wrote Juan

Leaving the Bucket

Ramon Jimenez—while marking potato rows I must pay attention.

The marker, a refashioned cultivator, sits behind the old Case tractor, with wings extending far from each side. As I make the first pass, aiming for a flag at the field's end, I lower the extension to the unfinished side of the field, and the wheel on the wing's end marks a line I will follow on the next pass. "Just pretend it's going up the crack of your ass," says a farmer wryly at the local café. "That'll make you drive straight." The boss's advice is more specific: use the hood ornament at the front of the tractor, align it with the mark extending the length of the field.

But if I look at the ornament, there are two lines, and if I look at the line, there are two ornaments. Called parallax, this phenomenon is how two eyes give us depth perception—though I do not know it at the time. Explaining my dilemma to the boss, he looks perplexed, laughs, and tells me to "figure it out," so I split the difference between the two visions, measure frequently to assess the rows' widths.

Making straight lines requires discipline and patience—or a fear that passersby will view any mistake. I drive slow, measure often, to make sure the "guess row"—where the two passes meet and all mistakes in width collect—is neither narrow nor wide, but the thirty-six inches required. Concentrating on the rows splitting my buttocks, my attention leaves its usual focal point—the future toward which I move.

Looking at that future I see one, two or many, depending on how far down my row I look. If I focus on the distant, my presents multiply like the tractor's hood ornament, if on the close, my futures do. If all points pass to the end of the row—death—it doesn't matter where I pass on that way, and if, shortening my focus by letting my imagination run wild, all futures become possible, my every move toward them becomes crucial. Depth perception aids us in the material world, is less useful in the realm of ideas.

If I need career or money or prestige I need the straight and uniform row. A specialized world requires specialized paths, having lost the flexibility of non-linearity. The pressure of either maintaining or failing such a path maddens me, so I drink to remove it from consciousness. Riding the wheel mark of my destiny as the tightrope walker walks his rope, I shift from sobriety to drunkenness, wavering, nervous and intent, and forever out of balance.

My guess rows are askew.

**

My niece Ashley, barely four, is pretending to read. She moves her lips as she turns the pages of a children's book. Noticing that I observe her, she says, "I'm not reading out loud." She points to her throat. "I'm reading in my mind."

We think of the mind as present in our head, perhaps because much of our sensory input arrives through eyes, ears, nose and tongue and is then processed in the brain. But this is only convention. In a study shedding light on that fallacy, experimenters fashioned human outer ears, and placed microphones where the ear canals would be, the same distance apart as real ears are. Connected by headphones to those ears, subjects experienced the center of acoustic space moving out of their heads to the space between the microphones. If another person placed his mouth between the two microphones and spoke, the voice moved from outside the observers' heads to inside. Mind moves, it seems, can as easily be in a child's throat, in a cat's tail or a lobster's claw. For Bateson it is almost everywhere in nature, and when we wrongly separate it as being only in the head our thinking goes awry.

Ashley's mind is in her throat and in the book she is reading. My mind oscillates between the workplace and the bar: I am not a farmer, I tell myself, I'm too good to be a manual laborer—my mind scoots off to the bar; I am not a drunk, I say, I'm above such vulgarity—my mind runs to the job; I am above both manual labor and drink—and that mind overwhelms me at home, alone, a bit of elusive mercury unassailable.

**

Writer-renegade C.L. Rawlins, working in the high mountains of Wyoming's Wind River Range, once measured the daytime winter temperature of conifer needles there at 92 degrees, due primarily to the sun's glare off the glazed, reflective snow. An hour later, after sunset, the air temperature read five below. "Conifers have mechanisms to keep ice crystals from piercing cell membranes, but these take time to work," he writes. "With nearly one hundred degrees of temperature drop in one hour, ice crystals form like tiny scalpels inside each cell." Every system has thresholds between which it operates, and beyond those constraints they may instantly "freeze" and explode. Chasing mind from place to place in the system called self, we addicts invariable go beyond those constraints, crippling ourselves much as the freezing pine.

**

The boss sends me down to American Falls for parts—parts which I have no name for nor can describe. I am embarrassed by my lack of knowledge, stand naked and judged as I use the parts house phone to call my employer, who explains in mere seconds to the parts man. Bearings, bolts, motors, speed chain—each have their own idiosyncratic method of measurement. Fine or coarse thread, lefts or rights, regular or metric, size sixty or fifty, half-links or whole, pillowblocks or needle, two-twenty or one-ten, with or without races—the jargon passes through my ears, does not stick.

I cannot speak the farmer's language of truck engines and transmissions, but I do speak the universal language of Dionysus. Worldwide, once one has imbibed sufficiently, the topics devolve to drinking and sex. The only "gringo" at the Mexican bar in Grandview, I converse nightlong with a few Spanish words and the unspoken agreement that the "wetbacks" and I are equals, sharing the same lives. I feel no embarrassment over my ignorance—Margarito

Leaving the Bucket

says my tongue is "more loose" when I'm drunk, a function of found confidence.

Language is a tool used on the medium of others' minds, others who color me as does any environment: our choppy sentences of mixed gutter English and pidgin Spanish, combined with the vulgarity slung at the bars, work and the coffee shop, change my manner of speech. Once believing myself learned, my speech no longer differs from the rural yahoos from whom I would wish to dissociate.

**

On some days, when the fields are too wet to till, we work in the shop, waiting for the ground to dry. I stare at the pool of oil below the drill press, where a hundred silver ribbonlike curls of steel lay. Across the floor sawdust patches soak up the dropped oil from transmissions, engines and pumps. In a corner of the shop, by the bathroom, stand buckets of solvent, cases of grease and gear oil. Nearby, on stands, are fifty gallon barrels of transmission oil, pump oil and engine oils of different viscosity. There is a table full of wheel line parts, distributor caps, fan belts, and projects partially underway. Nailed to the wall is a bolt bin full of nuts and washers and bolts of different lengths. The double-wheel grinder, the vise, and the welder sit in another corner, along with varying lengths and shapes of steel with which to strengthen or alter equipment.

The shop is dingy, dusty, dirty and dank, with only two windows less than two by three feet square in a building of nearly two thousand square feet. The four artificial lights are just one hundred watt bulbs, two of them shining from twenty feet high ceilings.

It is dark and oppressive. My lack of mechanical knowledge hangs in the air, heavy with dullness. I stand around for the most part, looking for simple tasks, as the "go-fer" or witless assistant. Agitated by my incompetence, I long for the minutes to pass more swiftly, for an excuse to work elsewhere, anywhere. I sweep the floor, arrange wrenches, stretching tasks to fill the hours. The boss's indifference to my discomfort worsens my sense of worthlessness.

**

The tractor drones as I drive up the hill, trying to find the mark hidden in the dust. The marker shifts behind me, taken by gravity, and I try to compensate by steering the tractor. In front, a killdeer drags its wing and walks frantically back and forth, pretending it is wounded in order to keep me from nearing its nest. I slow down, see the nest—a few pebbles and bits of straw on the barren ground, four eggs lying vulnerable in its confines. I raise the marker, drive past the nest, set the equipment back down. If a bird can confront an enemy outweighing it by a ten thousandfold factor, I can grant it reprieve, hope its eggs hatch before the planter comes by with a less merciful driver.

My rows bow on the ends. I edge the tractor over a few inches as I near the mainline, hoping to slowly remove the curve. A mistake of an inch at the first of the field can multiply into feet after a hundred passes.

Leaving the Bucket

On the last sweep through the field, I look back, read a sort of karma in the shape of those final rows. This tool is too clumsy for the scope of life I seek—I envy the killdeer, its courage and well-defined context.

**

Rain clouds appear on the horizon. The forecast says thirty percent chance of precipitation. I pray, hoping my thoughts form the attractors which the sky's water will form around, stir the calm into storm and end my workday by wetting the soil. Twelve days straight, twelve hours a day, I have sat on this tractor marking rows. Up and down, back and forth, the acres and minutes of my life passing.

The radio station adds to the monotony. Of all the songs written through all the years they can only play the same forty. Talk radio is worse, still more meaningless. I long for my own stereo, my own collection of music, and finally settle for silence. I shut off the stereo.

The diesel engine drones. The floor and windows vibrate. At the end of the field I raise the marker, do an "H" turn, maneuver to make the next pass.

Wind gusts stir the dust. I look back to check the marker's position, see the clouds ever nearer. I hold back my anxiety, so as not to be let down. Verga stains the horizon. A gray sheet of dust rolls in free from the desert, by my guess two miles away. A few raindrops hit the windows like spittle, cling to the blowing dust. I turn on the windshield wipers, smearing the glass. I wait for a moment to let the mud dry, then go outside with a paper towel and wipe the window clean.

Dust gathers on the wheels. Going north, I can see nothing behind me, the back window being covered with dirt. I stop the tractor at the field's end—my wait will soon be over. The thunderstorm will strike and end my day, or will pass and leave me still working.

Lightning hits nearby. There is a sudden crash of pelting rain. I shut down the tractor, grab my lunchbox and run for the pickup, hoping to get out of the field before the road gets too muddy.

**

I should go home, rest from the endless working days, but instead I head for the bar. There will be others there to share my like circumstances, glad to be out of their tractors and around people.

Already the beer flows, the mugs raise amidst shouts. I grab mine and sit with acquaintances. It goes down fast, as does the next and the next, the tone of the bar's atmosphere livening accordingly.

We eat beer nuts and pickled eggs, foregoing a supper, and play foosball until closing time. Ida tries to roust us out, and when finally she does, we sit in our cars drinking more. Jazz blasts out through the night, and having abandoned our lives for the moment, we fill the sky and the earth with the present. Mind seems ubiquitous, not only in our isolated selves.

We assume it will continue to rain, since clouds still obscure the stars. We will sleep in, relaxed, even with hangovers, change the pace of lives too frenzied.

**

Six A.M. The morning bursts through a cloudless sky and through my bedroom window. My tongue is dry, my head achy, my nerves already frayed, my heart racing. I can smell the rank cigarette smoke in my hair, the beer on my clothes where I have spilled.

I will get no day off, no extra sleep with which to salve my hangover. Instead I will get light and another day marking rows, following lines. The only thing worse would be to be stuck in the shop, in the dark and the dank of my ignorance.

This is my life: light where I do not want it, dark where I cannot stand it; endurance my only skill, addiction my only tool.

I rise only because I am able.

RELATIVITY, CATHARSIS AND HORIZONS

Just three years old, I point across the river toward the horizon and ask my mother what lies there, at the edge of the world—I don't understand why we never reach that edge, though we often drive or walk toward it. She tries to explain: "The Reservation is over there." But I mean *there*, at the edge, where sky meets the land and leaves the eye, not the place she imagines is beyond it.

Like that horizon, most boundaries recede from us as we near them. Selves and families, communities and nations, seem discreet, bordered entities, but searching their edges we find they blend into other, more complex systems. Only when we turn as Lot's wife did, look back at what we have left, do we sense its singularity and separateness. And then, our consciousness crystallizes as she did, petrified by our concretizing vision.

I grew up at the edge of things. The Snake River separated our family from the Shoshone-Bannock Indian Reservation, the school district stopped at our house, the phone district ended there, too. We wandered the perimeter of the local religion but never belonged. My mother was German, a war bride from the enemy, so I learned early—though taught otherwise—the illusory nature of national borders.

Just out of high school, I'm surrounded by a horizon as impenetrable as the blue dome of sky. What will I do now, and where will I go? Clearly I must leave to seek my fortune, but I have no blueprints to give me impetus. I hear news from beyond the sealed dome that is my upbringing, but one can plot and understand the stars' courses and still amongst them be unable to travel.

The dome hindering my movement, I discover years later, is the hard shell of pride. To go past the horizon I must enter the unknown and expose myself as a social illiterate. Barely able to make my way through the streets of Blackfoot, a town of less than ten thousand people, I find imposing the large cities where I must go to find what others call a life. Uncomfortable in others' presence, I am moreso in the company of strangers—reared in spaciousness and isolation, I have few social tools. Loathe to admit these and other shortcomings, I am too proud to submit to a context I don't understand.

My attention pressed to the edge of that context, I turn, find solace where possible—I park my life at Joe's Bar. Alcohol dims the apparent barriers, temporarily erasing my obsession with what I am not.

Bateson, in his seminal phenomenology of alcoholism, described alcoholic pride. To prove himself stronger than the bottle, the alcoholic must accept the dare to drink, and to stop drinking at any point is to admit losing to "John Barleycorn." The drinker puts himself in an impossible position, for he can only beat drink by taking the dare, and by doing so, loses. It is this impossibility that shapes alcoholism: one cannot stop the habit and still claim victory.

Bateson calls the alcoholic's relationship with drink *symmetrically schismogenic*, each agent escalating the behavioral ante until the system collapses. The bottle says "you can't beat me" and the drinker says the same, unable to back down without losing face. Arms races and childhood fights, where each side mimics the other's behavior but increases its intensity at each response ("My dad's bigger than yours"), inevitably end in some sort of collapse, often in violence. Each bout with the bottle ends the same, and, according to AA literature, the alcoholic must reach the bottom to begin "recovery."

**

A paving company foreman sits beside me at the bar and complains of the Indian help he must by law hire to get a road-building contract across the Reservation. Despite offering high, union-scale wages and benefits, he cannot keep his help working. They are off drinking, at pow-wow's or hunting and fishing.

In *Tally's Corner*, anthropologist Elliot Liebow examined a similar situation on a sixties streetcorner in Washington D.C.'s black inner city. Every day a truck came by the corner, looking for workers among the many unemployed men loitering there, but offered a job, most declined, though they had nothing else to do. Liebow summarized their reasoning thusly:

"The streetcorner man is under continuous assault by his job experiences and job fears... (which)...feed on one another. The kind of job he can get...steadily confirms his fears, depresses his self-confidence and self-esteem until finally, terrified of an opportunity even if one presents itself, he stands deflated by his experiences, his belief in his own self-worth destroyed and his fears a confirmed reality." To accept the job, he must admit need, and to have a job reminds him of his lowliness, even moreso than not having one.

Most of us at Joe's, though we may not admit it, share the attitude of the streetcorner blacks and the local Indians. However much we may need a better life and more money, we want to keep our life valued as is: to submit to the schedule and demands of work is to admit the insufficiency of our present lives—our only valued possession.

Through the world's eyes and mine I am a failure, but at Joe's I am on equal footing with others, known only as I am *here*. I have no past prior to my appearance at the bar and no future extending beyond. I'm not measured by what I drive or by how much money I make. My companions and I drink, share time, and back against back we shield ourselves from the ever-approaching horizon.

**

There is a highway to town, an interstate from there, an airport in Pocatello. But imagining myself there, I foresee more horizons, the unbreachable space between them and wherever I am. One hungover morning, willful to end my long-running sickness, I drive to town and buy traveler's checks. I leave a note for my parents saying I'm on the bus to Portland, stop at Joe's to say my farewells.

There, I have a beer.

And another.

And another.

The need to leave dissipates. My ill will toward myself and the conditions which made me what I am dissolve—I discover *place*. I am like Dostoevski's character Kirillov, who, redeemed, found that we all, if we but knew it, are happy—in alcohol's grip, I know it.

I have another drink.

A particle of light, I witness the passing waves, grow increasingly solid with each sip. The alcohol moves through my bloodstream, arranging my thoughts in a more pleasingly patterned manner. Oblivious to the world's movements, I watch instead the internal flow which seems to move without purpose. I listen to my companions at the bar: fluctuating potato prices, farmwives' sordid odysseys, interest but do not affect me. They are stories, just stories, this insignificant moment's expression of history's generalities. My horizon extended to include time's full vastness, I am placed in a field of possibility without limit. I know where I am in time, it does not matter where I'll be or where I've been. One can measure, physicists claim, a particle's position or its direction, but never can we know them both simultaneously; the same might be said about the self.

Leaving the Bucket

The horizon sinks into dusk. The world's edge is at once the tavern door and a place extending forever, where nothing lies beyond. Without *there*, the place where I should be, I am here, comfortable and grounded and placed. Equipped with ten hours worth of intoxicants, I step into an even broader, more open world.

I need no bus ticket away.

**

Einstein's theories suggest man cannot quite reach the speed of light, and that as one nears it the task grows increasingly difficult. While *we* cannot equal light's speed, the theory doesn't suggest it cannot be exceeded. It is only a barrier, a dome, and whatever travels faster than light has as much difficulty nearing it and slowing down as we do speeding toward it.

Barriers—women executives have their glass ceilings, I have my rural restraints. I must change, become less rural, women must become "un-womanlike"—we must become what we're not to be elsewhere, be elsewhere to become what we're not. The hyper-speed-of-light extraterrestrials share our horizon, but see it from a different angle.

Why change? Why break through a barrier if the barrier remains, why move to a horizon which forever shifts? Why go elsewhere if I have to lose what I am? Is wanting to change not a comment on one's own insufficiency?

Drunk, content with those questions, I defend my stationary position. But once sobered, I feel the necessity of movement—and, unable to move beyond the horizon, I instead get deeper into the world I inhabit: my self. After a dozen and a half beers, a few joints, a shot of tequila, a line of cocaine, I break that single barrier, pass successfully from quiet stoicism into a new, more vibrant persona.

Early in his career, Freud used the cathartic method to relieve his patients of long withheld emotions. A patient, often through hypnosis, can recall and re-experience repressed incidents and emotions in the safe environs of therapy, relieving himself of the symptoms the repressions caused.

Perhaps every drinker assumes his habit for alcohol's cathartic ability—the pent up feelings I must harbor while sober fountain out once I'm sufficiently drunk. Having passed the horizon of my quiet, sober self I am suddenly gregarious, at once giddy and amorous. I become wavelike, subject only—any observer can tell where I'm going (to unconsciousness) but not where at the moment I am. The world stands still; I move.

I race around the corner, behind the bar, and when girls pass by nab them by pulling my t-shirt over their heads. A beer in one hand, a fifth of whisky in the other, I jump on the bar and pretend to strip-tease. I sing rounds which the bar joins in with, shout obtuse jokes only I understand, no doubt amusing myself more than others.

Catharsis can cure only when the patient is properly distanced from the drama he re-enacts. If he remembers too vividly he simply re-lives it, thus imbedding the incident further, and if he recalls it too distantly he over-intellectualizes it—and knowing is

Leaving the Bucket

not doing. Watching my distancing self, careful to not reflect on the broader problems of tomorrow and yesterday, I simply bypass the necessary re-enactment. Later, unable to sustain the chase of mind away from self, I emote, but at too close a distance to solve my difficulties. Alcohol, a tool, requires a skilled user, and I am not of that handy ilk.

**

The universe is forever expanding, its pieces flung outward from the original "Big Bang." Despite our increasing distance from one another, occasionally an old friend stops in, reminding me of a pre-alcoholic time. The chance meetings bring to mind Einstein's thought experiment in which twins travel by separate trains. The twin on the train moving faster than light returns years later to find his sibling, who was travelling on a slower train, older than himself. The faster we move in time, Einstein claimed, the more slowly we will age.

As the older twin, I watch my friends whizzing by, grabbing careers and wives, caught in the world of *samsara* but aging less swiftly than I. They swing by, give reports of "out there," their voices sounding more distant, more different each time.

**

"I'm a lifer," I joke to Warren at the bar, who has returned from his job in Wyoming to visit family. It's simultaneously an explanation and an apology which

I commonly use when speaking to those who have managed to leave—my ironic self-awareness somehow lessens my stigmatic inertia.

Warren failed a couple grades in school, but still was able to leave, while I, the whiz kid, cannot. Friends, neighbor, family—they possess some magical key. Still others, keyless like me, go on unconcerned, inattentive to that smothering sky that recedes as we near it. I envy their contentedness, then despise their ignorance. We are all imprisoned, but only I seem to know it.

Space—the distance between edges, horizons, thresholds, between the walls of a country tavern. At a specific distance from a black hole not even light can turn back from its enormous gravitational pull. This "event horizon" is the last point where matter can escape. In the space beyond it, the black hole subsumes all, like the destruction of Sodom and Gomorrah taking with it Lot's curious wife.

After that tragedy, Lot's daughters slept with him so his seed might be passed on—but we cannot replace our brittle visions so easily. Once we witness our horizons' proclivity toward self-destruction, we cannot trust their singlemost strength: the sturdy shelter and foundation they supposedly provide. There can be no safety without shelter, one can find no catharsis without safety, and looking either forward or back I tremble at my conclusion: we are lifers, all, homebound between receding horizons.

HOW I SPENT MY CHRISTMAS VACATION

The Mexican boys wrestle for turns sitting beside me, touch the blonde hairs of my arm as if they might be sacred. They ask me English equivalents for their names, then tease each other with their new, foreign labels. The boxcar which serves as the village grocery fills with other onlookers as Margarito, Faustino and I drink lukewarm Coronas. When I turn to look at the eyes of those gathering, each averts his gaze and avoids my—the gringo's—glance.

This must be what it's like to be a circus sideshow.

After pressuring me for several years, Margarito has convinced me to deliver his newly bought pickup from Idaho to his home deep into Mexico, sparing him from the excessive tariffs he would incur if driving it himself. I thought I had again evaded him when he left the fields with his family in October, but with Christmas nearing he called to remind me of my oft broken promise. In a mixture of pidgin English and Spanish he gave me directions amounting to this: "Drive nine hundred miles, then turn left."

Despite considerable anxiety, I managed to find him with those minimal directions. Now that I am here, he insists I spend the winter—"*vacacion*," he says—but I want nothing more than to fly straight home.

**

Feeling as did Mark Twain, when he called vacations "an expensive way to be miserable," I can only infer what the millions taking them find pleasurable: they like being pampered, brought drink and food and play at every whim; they like seeing something new, feeling new sensations, having their nerve endings constantly titillated and thus escaping boredom; they enjoy getting away from the everyday, removing themselves from a routine become either too repetitive or too chaotic; or perhaps they like possessing an experience a friend may not have, thereby elevating their social status.

Of these possibilities, only "getting away" is not an obvious extension of ego. A desire to leave at least part of oneself behind, it is tragically impossible, for though on vacation we may temporarily escape routinized lives, eventually we run out of time or funds and must return to them. The word "tour" stems from the name of a tool used to ascribe a circle, and indeed a tourist must, like the circle, return to his starting point, the drudgery or anxiety whence he came, only to find its oppressiveness deepened—if he enjoyed his vacation, everyday life pales beside it, and if not, his hope of escaping normalcy dissipates.

So a vacation is a binge of sorts, an effort to leave one's life for something better, and like all binges, rather than sating desire creates it. Emerging hungover and jetlagged, we gain either a gaudy and flimsy framework against which to unfavorably compare normal life, or an increased hopelessness and a greatened need for another period of imbibing.

**

The 1979 Chevy's pinging engine sounds as worrisome as I feel, and I cross my fingers, pray we make it the two thousand miles to San Luis Potosi. I drive beneath the speed limit, watch the oil gauge diligently, unknotting on the long route through Nevada the logic committing me to this trek.

My family, isolated dairy farmers, never left the farm for periods longer than the few hours between milkings, and though my father ran off to Alaska as a youth, then spent seven years in the military gallivanting across the U.S. and Germany, I inherited the tools of comfort rather than his wanderlust.

A trip to town twenty miles away was a fearful and uncommon ordeal, and I had no interaction with others my age until the first traumatic day of school. Though no child raised by wolves, I found civilization alien, and consequently avoided novel sensations and excursions.

So I have lifelong been chastised as timid. Raised by three sisters, I was too well protected from challenge. Our distance from neighbors and town, the silence therein afforded, and the shadow of my siblings' care for me muted my reality, making any encounter outside it that much more vivid. And so assaulted, I often responded by crying when very young, retreating to books somewhat later, and finding intoxicants when I reached the age of that possibility.

I have long imaged within me a different self than this well-placed, placid one, one wishing to be freed and who, liking adventure, will be admired once he's unleashed. Long out of vogue, ever seeking to be in fashion, I have now, over the long period of negotiation with Margarito, painted the comfort-seeking self into a corner, forcing via the loyalty to my word an inchoate adventurer's unlikely undertaking. My cries will not alert my sisters, no book will free me from my incurred predicament, and drugs can only exacerbate my tensions. I am trapped.

So, regretfully I pass through Nevada's mining towns, their narrow streets. Gaudy Las Vegas, its plasticity looking just hours away from the dumpster. Spectacular Boulder Dam. The sprawl of Phoenix. A truck stop in Tucson that bears all the trappings of a state asylum.

At last, tired and hungry, I stop to eat in a small Texas town. Border patrol agents sit at the adjoining table, betraying my nearness to a foreign country. I instinctively try to look normal, hide my illegal activity, though I know they have no interest in my minor offenses. I find a motel room, bed down early, hoping to savor a final night of familiarity.

**

The Oxford Dictionary defines vacation as "a rest from some occupation, business or activity," while a related word, vacate, can mean "to render inoperative, meaningless or useless." We might construe a vacation, then, as an absence of meaning—an absence often coming when we require its presence most.

Modern philosophers insist man instinctually seeks novelty, but it might be better said that he craves information, which Bateson defined as a "difference that makes a difference." Few can sit idle for long, needing both to act and be acted upon in a dialogue best understandable as an exchange of information.

Some have interpreted this need as evidence of man's inherent aggressive nature, a link to his violent animal ancestry, and have utilized their interpretations to justify social coercion. Erich Fromm, while agreeing man was by nature aggressive, believed this instinctual force creative rather than animal, taking violent form only when thwarted or twisted.

But the need lies deeper than creativity, aggression or a quest for novelty—we need to exchange with the world, be involved in the Tao, its continuous informational flow. When we feel the space between us and the world widening too far, we sense a vague impulse which we interpret in different ways—some consume, some create, some are violent, but all must experience the world or be experienced, to readdress life's meaning by re-connecting to its dissipating patterns.

Using Bateson's definitions, we must rule out trivia for the sating of this basic desire. Like a candy bar to the starving or a lottery ticket to the homeless, it masquerades as something more substantial than it is—we receive the momentary impression that our need has been sated, but an instant later find ourselves left with only more need. Trivia may be a difference, but it makes no difference.

The information man requires instead hinges upon meaning—the depth of which vacations rarely render. Though we often go on vacation to seek new information, to fill the gap we sense created in our beings, we generally meet only trivia there, a series of meaningless differences—another postcard, another sensation, another fine meal, another picturesque scene. Like the drunken night which was to transform us, lift us from our drudgery, the vacation gives us only another empty—vacant—spot in our memory, one filled with needy shouts of "*una mas*"—one more.

**

Anxious, unable to sleep, I leave town at four in the morning and reach the Mexican border well before noon. I immediately encounter the corruption everyone hears about—it takes twenty dollars to bribe Margarito's television and stereo past the Juarez border guard, another twenty for his assistant, who "gots keeds to buy presents for, too." Miles further, at the next inspection station, the agent there will shake his head when I explain my lack of papers, but will let me through despite my cargo's illegal, untariffed status.

Onto foreign streets, I at once take a dead end—and another—searching out a service station for fuel. I see none of the brands I'm accustomed to—no Chevron or Amoco or Standard, no Gulf or Sinclair or Maverick—so turn back through the city, perplexed.

Leaving the Bucket

I drive through again, at last see what must be the only gas station—the nationalized chain, Pemex.

Too proud to ask for directions there, I search out traffic signs, see a one by two foot sign pointing the way to Mexico City. But the road seems to go deeper into the suburbs, so I turn back whence I came.

Back at the border, I am accosted by several youths on foot, wishing to wash my windows. I give one a dollar, and he directs me to a road heading south, out of the city.

Beyond Juarez, the terrain seems a wasteland of poverty, with decrepit buildings, dirty streets and windowless homes. Unaccustomed to such squalor, assuming it will only get more hell-holeish the further I go, I consider turning back. But I have two tasks to perform—deliver Margarito's pickup, television and stereo, and prove to the internal critic that indeed I can step outside myself.

The fool wins out, again.

The poverty slowly clears as I leave the shadow of the U.S., giving me fodder for pondering our neighborly influence.

**

I look for a place to buy food, but can find no convenience stores, no restaurants, no shopping centers, so settle for a sixpack of Coke from a dirty taco cart at the edge of Chihuahua. Only when I reach Margarito's will I realize that the cardboard 7-

up and Coca-Cola advertisements I pass along the way designate shops where one might purchase groceries.

In Chihuahua, I discover I have chosen a bank holiday for my foray, so my traveler's checks are useless until the next day. I count my American money—only enough for gas. It will be a long drive with no sleep or food—all the rest of the day, all the night.

I fuel up, ask for directions—which take me to the city center, another dead end. Once more I try, this time spot a sign which says TRUCK ROUTE, which I follow around the outskirts. American truck routes shorten one's drive, but this one winds, loops and snakes at twenty miles per hour. Two hours later I reach the open road past Chihuahua. Having been twice stranded in Mexican cities, having more time than room for anxiety over being lost, I will take the truck routes around the remaining cities, all of them taking like time.

The road blurs. Just an extension of the North American desert, the landscape looks much like Idaho and Nevada, save a tropicalization of the vegetation. Dry, parched, plants distantly distributed, few towns, and almost no streams or rivers.

My Spanish, adequate in Idaho fields with those accustomed to an American accent, increasingly falters the further south I go. In Juarez, in Chihuahua, I can make myself understood, but by Zacatejas and Torreon my pronunciation meets only puzzlement. The worth of a dollar goes down, my foreign status becomes more pronounced, and my caffeine buzz conjoined with a rising anxiety electrifies the enveloping world.

Leaving the Bucket

**

Europeans call vacations "holidays"—holy, restful days—but most Americans think of them as empty containers, cramming as much sensation into them as possible. We race about Ireland in a week, with a checklist of sites to see, when a European may spend the same time walking a small area in a single west coast county. Our hunger for information is stronger, our likelihood of being misdirected by trivia far greater.

Comedians and psychologists alike have long accrued ample resources for their trade from the American family vacation. Intended as an escape from a stressful relationship, such a trip often only compresses the dynamics and tensions the travelers seek to avoid, for if brother hates sister at home, he hates her worse in the more confined station wagon, where there is no contact with others to lessen and deflect the tensions.

Unfortunately, I discover, a vacation alone does likewise, exacerbating internal tensions I wish to leave. With nothing to distract me from my stigmata, I can attend to little else. Each time I consider stopping for a drink or a break, then fearfully talk myself out of it and watch the possibility pass, I relive the tensions of stasis against chaos, the wish for pleasure warring with the desire to avoid pain, the stolid and placid self throttling the adventurer.

That adventurous, imagined self is not emerging from its confining shell, judging from my lack of enjoyment on this lengthening excursion. I cannot will myself free of self without strengthening that self—it is a paradox which I'd hoped this drive might annihilate.

**

Night. The narrow highway, shoulderless, snakes through hills and valleys. A fifteen mile ribbon of tail lights tells me where I will be in twenty minutes. The traffic is comprised almost entirely of trucks, most of them decades old, and many have replaced their typical yellow, white and red clearance lights with the blues and greens denoting the nearing holiday. It is a long, surreal string of Christmas lights, stretching through a night that tails off forever.

I have driven for nearly twenty hours now, am tired from the constant winding. I nod off between towns, wake as I pass slowly through the narrow streets, the village walls that must be centuries old. I stop alongside the road when I can go no further and try to sleep. But stopped, I am suddenly alert, so begin again for a few more wearying miles.

The well-lit tractor dealerships at the edges of towns tell me I'm in farming country—though I see no farms. Occasionally I see a communist sickle painted on a bridge abutment. I pass trucks full of tropical fruit, wonder where I am heading. At almost every village I pass there is a small cinderblock building with the word "VULKA" stamped on its side, and I spend the hours mystified, trying to translate the unlikely sounding word. Later, I will be told it denotes a tire repair shop—vulka, from vulcanized rubber.

Leaving the Bucket

There is alienness even in this alien tongue.

**

My bowels, weak and watery, fed only by a six-pack of Coke during the past twenty-four hours, cry for emptying, but there are no rest stops. Instead, from time to time a small road veers alongside for a hundred feet, and there, judging from the thousands of piles of excrement and toilet paper, travelers relieve their needs.

I stop at one, but sickened, grasp hold of my callings and drive on. But need strikes again and I stop—and again I refrain. But finally my bowels will not hold. Nearly dawn now, I drive off the highway, tiptoe gingerly through the fly-ridden piles, and, gagging in the absence of manners, squat and leave as quickly as possible.

**

Freud posited the internal war between caution and recklessness as man's life instinct, or quest for novelty, battling his death instinct, the urge toward stability. We wish things to be the same, then wish them to be different, and the war between these two impulses we call the self. It is an insoluble problem, for if all was new we could not exist sanely, having no ground beneath us, and if all stayed the same there could be no change, no movement of life, only death. We shuffle between these two poles, always uneasy, evading first change, then sameness.

In our era the new complexity scientists state the problem somewhat differently on a cosmic scale, seeing the *fitness* of any system—species or self or group of planets—as being in a narrow range between complete order and total chaos. In that range, they believe, lies complexity, where order and chaos reign together in a tenuous (im)balance. Fit systems survive because they approach criticality—the edge of chaos—without going over, while the unfit either fail to approach or pass beyond it.

The question which is best—order or chaos--, then, is not answered by selecting one over the other, but by discovering how much order serves best in relation to the chaos in one's life—what allows one to best survive. Traditional religion's teachings of moderation seem oddly appropriate.

In Anne Tyler's *The Accidental Tourist*, the protagonist is a finicky, anal retentive author who writes books for businessmen on how to endure their travels, make distant places more like home. Detailing the hotels most like America's, the restaurants serving food most like home, Macon, systematic and rational to the extreme, is chastised by Sara, the wife who has left him: "...there's something so...muffled about the way you experience things, I mean love or grief or anything; it's like you're trying to slip through life unchanged. Don't you see why I had to get out?"

He replies,"Sara, I'm not muffled. I...endure."

"Travel" and "travail" were once the same word, both of them perhaps agonies to be endured. If life is a traveling, a vacation between the two points of birth and death, perhaps Macon is right to simply endure it. For Macon—and for me—one of two questions seems to frame every man's action—why? Or why not? If we ask the latter our impulse is to leave the status quo, find novelty; if the former, it is to stay and resist change.

And endure.

**

I near San Luis Potosi. Soon my ordeal will be over. The smaller towns pass: Ahuahulco, Agua Prieta. By Margarito's directions, Agua Luco—the place I am to turn left at—is close. I look for a service station—he said stop at "caseta sero," which translates as station Sero (Sero, I assume, being the name of the station's owner). From there someone will be posted to show me the rest of the way.

I lift my weary eyes, try to attend to every sign. But suddenly I am already inside San Luis Potosi's—a city of a quarter million—outer limits. I have driven too far.

I question my appraisal, for I have been watching the signs very carefully. I could not have missed Agua Luco. So I drive on, thinking Margarito's directions somehow askew. Getting deeper into the urban area, however, I realize I must turn around. I drive twenty miles north, retrace my route.

Again I find myself in the city. I return to the outskirts, stop at a food cart at the city's edge, and the shy girl operating it, though refusing to look me in the eye, guides me back where I came.

I follow her directions, driving more slowly, watching more intently the sides of the highway—perhaps Agua Luco is smaller than the tiny towns I pass. I stop where I first suspected the village should be, twenty miles out, and unable to see the town I again lose hope.

I stop at a church near Ahuahulco—the nuns can tell me nothing. A café owner across the highway gives me similar information, and suggests I rest with him, share a glass of wine. I find a service station in Ahuahulco, am elated, hoping it to be Caseta Sero, but they too have no help for me—not even a phone. I must be close, but I have no idea of how to get closer.

Disheartened, I realize I may have to drive back without having found Margarito—my ordeal all for naught. But I am too tired to panic, too wound with willpower to surrender just yet. I must stop, gather my thoughts and consider alternatives. I will phone someone back in the United States who might have a number or address of one of Margarito's relatives or friends—several work near where we do back in Idaho.

In Ahuahulco, I stop in front of a little shop with the international telephone symbol hanging above the door, try to decide who to call. I breathe deeply, retrieve my wits, measure my possibilities. Margarito has no phone, I haven't his address. I lean my head against the steering wheel, hopeless.

Suddenly, a young woman runs from the telephone building, shouting the same words again and again. She waves a piece of paper at me. I start—it's my mispronounced name she is yelling over and over—Margarito has just called. From her slowly enunciated Spanish I gather I must wait, that someone will come and guide me to his home. Caseta Sero, it turns out, means station zero—telephone operator. And Agua Luco is Ahuahulco.

Relief.

**

Bernadino's burro brays each dawn from across the yard, along with a crowing cock. My bed linens are damp from a heavy dew I wouldn't expect in a desert climate. The house smells of cement, as if the cinderblocks have just been laid—which unbeknownst to me they have. I am without bath for four days now, antsy in my skin—today I'm promised one in a wash tub I can barely sit in.

I sit to breakfast. Little is familiar here—though the Kellogg's rooster blares off the front of a Corn Flakes box, just like home. Only corporate America, its insignias emblazoning walls and signs, has accompanied me. I eat, as Margarito's new television blares American re-runs dubbed in Spanish.

We drive to Potosi to buy tubing so we can install the water heater. We take backroads through the tall desert vegetation which I could never retrace on my own. We park in the city center, are by my standards harassed there by a group of men in their twenties, but Margarito and his family seem unfazed. Across the broad downtown plaza, a Chinese restaurant larger than any I have seen in the U.S. cries out to be sampled, but my companions have no desire for such cuisine. We instead lunch inside an open two story mall filled with tiny shops. There, the "fresh" fish in the center of the mall exudes its freshness thirty yards, and the hawker spots my white skin and red beard and hails me from that distance.

After a bland Mexican meal we walk downtown. Margarito offers to buy me sidewalk wares—coconut milk, cactus fruit, new boots—but riddled with tenseness and fear I answer him with cautious but certain "no's"—hating myself intensely as I do so, but unable to break the tightened grip of self.

We finish our task swiftly, return via a different set of backroads. The sensations of the locale crowd together. The village's Catholic Church, its odd, part-Kremlin style architecture. An old woman leading a burro, huge clay pots full of *pulque* slung across its back. Succulents abounding, grass absent save on schoolyard soccer fields. Boundaries lined with cactus, shoulder to shoulder spines. Cement block walls separating properties, broken bottles atop them, clearly stating the nature of local trust.

Wrought iron gates, barefoot children, girls in pale dresses hiding behind every door, Margarito's open cesspool, *maguey* and skinny dogs and roofless homes and rutted roads and a single string of Christmas lights on a neighboring home and the white dust on the village paths and the solitary rabbits scooting through—

Enough.

I grab a beer at Margarito's—sip, breathe, the air and beer calming me. Embrace the sensations, says the critic, as I absorb the familiar ones of oxygen and alcohol. I lean back in the winter sun bearing down on Margarito's home and try to select which other ones to allow in. Having been far from myself before, I know how easily it is to be lost and overcome by the outside world. To say "yes" to all is to acquiesce, to be passive and extinguish the self, while saying "no," though a negating activity, extends the boundaries of will. One must stand one's ground somewhere or be lost.

The root of "passive" is the Latin word for suffer, and to truly experience otherness we must be passive—if we are active in a new environment we experience not it but ourselves. Vacations, then, must be suffered, if their novelty is to be acquired, but we enjoy them only when we experience ourselves more vividly.

Clever, says the critic, but most likely an excuse. I drink on, extinguishing the debate.

Faustino walks over from the other side of the village. We drive to the *tienda*, buy more beer, and drink for hours and share joints at Margarito's.

As the sun nears its rest we drive Faustino home, where he offers me peyote. I decline, glad he has not waited a couple more beers to ask me, when my defenses will be further eroded. I contemplate going mad under peyote's spell two thousand miles from home, in a place where I cannot speak the language, and ease back, grateful, as if having dodged a tragic bullet.

In the morning we breakfast with coffee at the kitchen table. Margarito's relatives—sisters-in-law, father-in-law, brothers—parade by, graciously making my acquaintance. Both Margarito and his father-in-law offer beautiful Celestina in marriage, and uncertain if it is in jest, I make sidestepping replies.

To critics of a stultified lifestyle I offer this: would you take these offered steps—the new experience of peyote, an unknown spouse taken at random—and thus end your life as you presently know it?

So, you have your threshold, too.

**

I am uneasy in Margarito's hospitality. He has moved his bed into a room for me while he and his wife sleep on the floor. Esperanza fixes my meals, ingratiatingly taking account of my vegetarianism. Margarito supplies me with beer, offers to buy me clothes, boots, a night at a concert. He seeks to satisfy my every whim—but I would be more inclined to stay if he would but give me time and space, act as if I were not here, but he understands reclusiveness no better than those I have left.

I tell him its Christmastime, I must be home to my family, and after much haggling he agrees to let me go. "Ralph no like Mexico," he says. I insist otherwise, but he refuses to believe me. I feel badly he thinks his country a poor host, but I am unable to explain my need for solitude, distance, sameness. He has made the same trek into the unknown for several years now, without the amenities I've been offered and for much longer periods of time, so how could he understand my squeamishness?

Leaving the Bucket

We buy a plane ticket in San Luis, drive out to an empty airport. We wait for the flight to San Antonio—the only flight all day, so far as I can see—but I am refused passage for reasons I cannot comprehend.

Margarito tries to bully the clerk, and I tense, afraid he'll intrigue higher authorities, who will jail me for illegally delivering untariffed goods. He comes back, explains the problem as best he can: I could be a murderer on the lam, says the clerk, so must check in with the authorities downtown.

I grin inwardly at the irony—timid me, a murderer.

**

We sidestep the authorities. We cash in the plane ticket, buy me a bus ride north. In eight hours the bus for Juarez and El Paso leaves. Margarito says farewell and I wait, nervous and alone, hoping I don't miss my ride back to sanity. A Mexican youth who speaks English stops to talk to me. He was at the airport when I was refused my flight, and tells me the plane suffered mechanical problems and didn't fly, anyway.

I thank him for the information, try to read. But every bus that pulls up outside draws my attention—I worry it's mine, that I may miss it. I fear being stranded halfway round the world, not knowing how to get back even to Margarito's village.

**

A cross above the bus's rearview mirror has been wired to the stereo's equalizer. It's multiple lights blink off and on to the bass notes of the Mexican music—Jesus leg, Jesus arm, Jesus head; thump, thump, thump: the stigmata of modern existence. I pick up words from the bouncy songs, drinking and loving their popular themes.

I try to read a work on mysticism, Ken Wilber's *Transformations of Consciousness*, but I've not the imperturbability necessary to shut out internal distractions. The book lends me none of the patience I hoped it would, just reminds me of my unenlightened nature.

The bus driver has been awake for at least twenty four hours—twelve less than me. When other busses pass, their overworked drivers honk, gesture vigorously with varying signals—perhaps their way of keeping one another awake. At each of the many stops a hard luck case asks for money or tries to sell gum, and from my front seat I avoid their desperate gazes.

As we near the border checking station, I grow increasingly worried. Will they spot me, check my papers, refuse my passage as they did at the airport? Will they send me back to Margarito's to either spend the winter or return with his pickup?

The pre-border station waves the bus by—only the border left to cross.

**

The American border guard at El Paso searches me, eyes me evilly, suspicious of my beard and slightly

Leaving the Bucket

long hair. He runs my license through the computer, feels inside my boots, asks me why I tremble. I hate him for noticing my fear, explain I've not eaten for over a day.

I can feel his contempt for me. It is almost as deep as my own.

**

Unchanged, save for an influx of relief, I arrive back home. My sixteen seat airplane tries twice to land in heavy Pocatello fog, one that holds thick down to three feet off the ground. After coming within inches of landing in an adjoining stubblefield, the pilot informs us we have enough fuel to try another landing or fly to Idaho Falls, where skies are clear.

Unanimously, we vote the latter.

I am unmoved. What is this, but one more novel ordeal.

**

Tyler writes: "It occurred to (Macon)...that the world was divided sharply down the middle: some lived careful lives and some lived careless lives, and everything that happened could be explained by the difference between them."

I have made my attempt at carelessness, received a joy equivalent to holding on to an electric fence for ten days. My tour, my circle, complete and suffered, I have extended myself but feel no more deeply than before. I am shouting, "I CAN DO IT, TOO!" but already the internalized critics have moved to new terrain.

I will never catch up—*they* will always be one step ahead, daring me like John Barleycorn. Once I have joined them, they will move on, prove they are not me and I not them. It is a variation of the fashion game—I am the outdated one defining what is not "in."

"Fashion," Abby Hoffman once noted with irony, "is right behind 'fascist' in the dictionary." The terror of not belonging drives us to join fads, groups, nations, in which we follow those possessing a different fear—not being adored.

But we do belong—wherever we are, whatever we wear. "Without leaving his home, the sage knows the whole universe," reads the Tao Te Ching—the principles underlying detail remain the same wherever one goes; we are connected, though we may not know it. The well-versed vacationer claims otherwise, indicates self-altering differences at every distant corner—differences to patch the holes in our lives that make us feel separate—but upon scrutiny we can see he has as many pre-set principles and rhythms as the stay-at-home he ridicules. Having traveled extensively he simply understands changing contexts—knows where to eat and where to go, is able to assimilate odd occurrences and circumstances not from instinct but from practice. Just as a good athlete recognizes possibilities, or a thinker intuits a place where arguments might be synthesized, the vacationer sees a pattern he can complete. Put him in a place where he has no grasp of the language, no link to a telephone or his bank account, no feel for the local customs—remove his comfort, his ground, give him a different game—and he too will feel the terror of being lost, of not belonging.

Let him marry a stranger and eat peyote.

**

At the airport in Idaho Falls I call my father to pick me up. A fellow passenger on the aborted flight has an unset broken leg suffered in an accident somewhere back east, and no way to get to Pocatello, his intended destination. We offer him a ride halfway there, to Blackfoot, where a friend has agreed to meet and pick him up.

Obviously in severe pain, he cringes at every bump in the road, and I ask why he didn't see a doctor when he broke his leg. "I just wanted to get home," he moans, "as fast as I could. I knew they would keep me in the hospital if I stayed."

I imagine his eagerness to be home, to there leave the weight of what must be a long endurance. I murmur my concurrence, as a like tenseness ebbs too slowly from within me.

HABITS

The Aberdeen-Springfield Canal was built near the turn of the century, in good part with mule teams pulling scrapers. At noon of the long workday the laborers stopped for a prepared lunch, and it's said the mules halted without prompting precisely at that hour, not budging even if the lunch whistle had not blown. Mid-stride, mid-load, as regular as the German philosopher Kant—by whose daily walk the villagers could set their clocks—the mules had come to habit and dutiful rhythm.

Seventy years later, parked on the canal bridge just a couple hundred yards behind Joe's Bar, I unscrew the cork from a bottle of wine. Beside me, Johnny deftly rolls a joint. We are, like the mules, expressing one sort of habit, but unlike them trying to break two greater ones—a task Kant may have insisted impossible. He believed those two habits, our senses and our reason, color our perceptions so strongly that rather than truly apprehending a *ding an sich*—a thing in itself—we only witness its appearance, as phenomena.

I take a drink, peer out over the bridge railing. The canal's craggy bottom lies exposed by the winter chill—rocks protrude, small basins stipple its surface, dried and frozen moss blankets what thin sheets of ice do not. Divested of the summer's river water, the canal is just one phenomenon overlying another more honest. It is a surface assumed real, a habit experienced so long that its users believe it inherent, even instinctual, as it ebbs and flows through two counties, a banked and seasonally emptied artery of human agriculture.

Johnny's Italian grandparents and their relatives settled here not long after the canal was built. Westward from here, the Beninis and DeGiulios and Drogheis own most of the rock ridden land—clear to the unfarmable desert. It's said that when asked why they chose such poor farmland, they reply it reminds them of whence they came. I suspect other reasons, perhaps there being no better land left.

**

Drugs and alcohol alter the senses, change and sometimes erase one's reason. My and Johnny's affection for mind-altering substances is nothing new—from the Hindus' with their *soma* to the Native Americans' with peyote, men have imbibed so they might witness the noumenal realm Kant claimed they couldn't. Some users believe they succeed, while others think their mystical reports to be just further alteration, a yet greater distortion of an already distorted reality.

I trade the wine for Johnny's hand-rolled joint, inhale and hold the tainted air. Perhaps both camps are right—sometimes lucidity appears, but as often confusion reigns. Seeking the sacred, to see as God must, we utilize what tools we are given—and fail or succeed accordingly.

Never having taken up cigarettes, my lungs unaccustomed to smoke, I cough, release the used atmosphere.

I pass Johnny the joint. Behind us, over in Gaelard's, as in many places along the canal, Russian olive trees grow wildly. A hard wood, it must be sawn when green—a chain saw won't cut through it once it's seasoned. Sparks fly, smoke rises, the air is filled with the odor of burning wood, but the cut through the yearly rings progresses slowly, if at all.

But when sawn into manageable pieces when green, then seasoned, Russian olive burns hot and clean in comparison with other woods. Its grain is unmatched in beauty but rarely used for aesthetic purposes—if not trained and pruned, the tree's gnarly character and dissuading thorns provide only short bits of useable wood. Few people, if any at all, do such pruning.

In *Sand County Almanac,* Aldo Leopold used a lightning stricken bur oak as a metaphor for his local history, and detailed the years passing as he sawed backward through its rings, through time. The history here, all Russian olive and seasoned on the stump, is less eagerly revealed to the sawyer.

**

The canal is full from the middle of April, when the first beet seedlings need water, to nearly the end of October, when potato harvest is complete. For the six months with water, the land within the canal's reach emulates a non-desert clime, but during the six

Leaving the Bucket

months without it returns to its arid nature. Still, in the winter with the ground barren, frozen and often snowless, no one can discern that natural character—around homes, non-native deciduous trees stand with bare branches and the evergreen pines grow plentifully enough to obscure their foreign status; the fields are either stubble or furrow, betraying none of the erased historic flora. Without more obvious evidence, we forget we live in a comfortable fiction.

Downstream from the Pingree bridge a couple miles, my grandparents homesteaded just off Taber Road, not far from the community of Springfield. Seeking an irrigated fiction, they raised alfalfa seed and cattle on the rocky, almost inarable land. On miserable summer days their sons walked the hundred yards to the canal and skinny-dipped to evade the harsh desert heat—their naked pre-teen bodies now appear in a photograph on the Post Office wall, where bits of local history hang pieced together.

I never learned to swim, though I grew up just a few miles away on the bank of the Snake River—which feeds this and other canals. Life, to my mother, was more precious than living, and she kept her children alive by instilling fear of the swift river water. I walked its banks frequently, watched from my upstairs window as it changed through the year—freezing over in hard winters, swelling with spring run-off, narrowing to a trickle during drought--, but never did I dare penetrate its surface.

Once I passed the age of accidental drowning, my mother recanted her warnings, insisting I take swimming lessons. But my fear had outpaced my sensibilities, and having found my will I refused by running away from home. She did not call my bluff.

But a few years older, increasingly shamed by my lack of a basic human skill, it was my turn to recant. With insufficient courage to admit my shortcoming by being taught to swim, but gathering enough to teach myself, I walked to a pond far out in the pasture where overflow irrigation water collected. I stripped, strode slowly toward the depths. The water covered my ankle, my knee, thigh, waist—then suddenly I lost my footing. Unable to gain my balance in the strange medium, I panicked, flailed wildly, and at last was able to stand. Once I calmed myself, I stepped very slowly toward the bank, praying I might make it back alive.

Afterward, certain I'd escaped a lonely and tragic death, I avoided any events near beaches or swimming pools, did not join companions at water outings. My life revolved about that single fear and hiding it from all those who knew me.

**

We cannot know a thing in itself, nor can we see history except through our senses and reason. Who, besides the original Italians, really knows how or why they arrived? Even they might be unaware of their motives, may disguise them with socially acceptable reasons. We *accept* our stories, our histories, our perceptions, only by keeping our vision focussed and narrow.

One must tread history like water. Otherwise, we drown in the fluidity of its perspectives. But just as

Leaving the Bucket

I am unable to swim, I cannot move through history. I know now one must not flail, must go instead with the flow, but still the years do not yield to my will—this backeddy, these habits, these addictions take me deeper, allow no passage beyond a recurring present.

A whirlpool: movement, making no progress—this is my interpretation of noumena, of which each self is a center. Only purpose gives an impression of progress—take that away from any time-line and everything turns to eddies. The whirlpool's double expression, its simultaneous nature of change and no-change, may reveal truth, God and the sacred, but it gives no meaning to the everyday, facilitates no future, no career, no history.

The canal is empty. It broke here at the bridge early last summer, sending water through the Pingree townsite and flooding Joe's Bar. Ida received a settlement of well over ten thousand dollars for damages to the seventy year old structure—more than the building's value, many claim.

The check was more sizeable than any she'd seen before, and it flowed as swiftly and broadly as the flood water that spawned it. A goodly portion she spent on building a much needed foundation and she bought a good stereo for the bar, but the rest disappeared in just weeks—to creditors, friends and the numerous hands in the till. The more conservative customers shake their heads disapprovingly, forgetting why they love Ida—no matter what she has, she naively passes it along, her transparent goodwill impenetrable but fluid.

She is an eddy, too. A whirling dervish of a woman going nowhere. When Johnny and I left the bar just minutes ago, she had her hand, as always, sharing several projects—wrapping a present for Aunt Jenny, rearranging junk on the walls, in the midst of cleaning both her apartment and the bar. As clientele, we revolve more slowly about her and the bar, but will unite at the center of the vortex in a few short hours.

**

Histories wish to be read. Some conifer seeds require excessive heat to explode their hard shells and reveal the genetic history within—the hardened, Russian olive soul needs something equivalent to soften its reluctant grain, that another might witness its internal workings and rings.

I finish off the bottle; the roach sits on my ashtray. The marijuana—supposedly Hawaiian *sinsemilla*—has taken new form in our cells. The sky and land seem more brilliant in appearance, our heads pulse with attentiveness—Johnny suggests we head over to Toad's and I concur, knowing we'll eventually circle back to Joe's.

We take the gravel backroad, drive further out on the desert. On Taber road we pass an old junkyard filled with rusted cans and bedsprings—leavings from the earliest settlers, perhaps even Johnny's grandparents. Occasionally, strangers with metal detectors come here, having been given a "treasure map" with their purchases. If they dig, for what they

Leaving the Bucket

hope is not more junk, they find a different sort of treasure—a geological history.

The topsoil here is but inches thick and alkaline. Below it, a hardpan of clay resists penetrations. A plow will not sink through it without considerable additional force, will instead ride along scraping its surface. A shovel merely recoils as it strikes the hard, white shale, chipping small, pale slivers from the clay.

But once a tool—be it ripper or plow or chisel—passes through the hard layer, it can be driven perpendicular to easily shatter the clay stratum. It may then reach gravel or sand below, or yet another layer of topsoil—all evidence of far earlier eras.

One sometimes finds arrowheads loosened aboveground in the dust, where drivers have passed thousands of times, enough to release them from history; along the reservoir cliffs, at a depth of nearly twenty feet, one can see pre-historic remains—past Aberdeen is a cross-section of bone sixteen feet long, what surely must be a massive, ancient animal's ribs. But searching the desert for history, such offerings are rare, just punctuation in a far broader silence.

We cannot know a thing, but perhaps a thing can know itself—perhaps, even, a self may know its own being. A kind act might surface, like a loose arrowhead, a memory may be revealed like a mastodon's ribs. Drink loosens the tongue, the tongue loosens the soul, the history, the strata, the imbedded.

Most addictions begin with some imbedded artifact, some pain about which they form—not joy but joylessness, wrote Nietzsche, is the mother of debauchery. A wound may infect, may then scar, may lay hidden for the life of the sufferer, but with alcohol or drugs—or even religion—he tries to expel the affliction. That failing, he uses the same tools in a different manner, to callous over the offending and painful sliver.

**

Toad isn't home—is partying, undoubtedly, elsewhere. My grand-aunt and uncle, devout Mormons who built this house, would be aghast at my friends dwelling here now. Danielson Springs, less than fifty yards away, was where my father was force-baptized in their zealotry.

Up on the hill, where still other partiers live, Grandma—a staunch Mormon, too—had to hide the bottle from my Grandfather. Most of my uncles had a similar feel for alcohol, and I hear as I traipse through the county—from old drinkers committed to their lifelong habits—of my father's carousing, as well.

"The saw works only across the years," wrote Leopold, "...the wedge, on the other hand, works only in radial splits...(yielding) a collective view of all the years at once." I cannot cut across the rings of a well-seasoned Russian olive, but I can sink an ax or wedge across its grain. For Leopold, a good history required all three tools—the ax, wedge and saw—to give an accurate and fair perspective.

As with the clay hardpan, the olive grain can only be broken easily if I come at it from the side—one enters a thing, a history, a self in the way each allows.

Leaving the Bucket

But sinking an ax in wet wood, one may be unable to retrieve it—the wood, rather than splitting, absorbs the ax. Marriage, family, commitments seem like wet wood, one's self being irretrievable once it penetrates them. So, sober and reasonable, I choose my stump carefully, put my ax only where I know it will return—there is no such place.

Caution, the junction of fear and reason, restrains the self from dangerous action. But any action presents danger, so caution must be overcome—alcohol and drugs provide that service. Once bereft of reason, with senses altered, chance can rear its axhead and let it fall where it might.

If you do not enter history—marriage, family, career—you cannot know it. If you do not step into the pond, you certainly need not swim. Drugs remove reason, smooth over fear and caution, allow one to be swept into history.

**

The canal, the railroad, the highway: in a space of only a couple hundred yards, three rings of a community's history. Further downstream the three have more distance between them, but here they are knotted by the engineers' whims. There are places in any self where its history lay just as knotted, places lying equally close to the surface, yielding slowly to the saw and not at all to the ax. We cluster at these places, perhaps hoping to find answers, perhaps just content being near them, however difficult they may be to perceive as things in themselves.

Joe's Bar sits between the tracks and the canal, an arrowhead imbedded in Pingree's history, and Johnny and I are back at Joe's amidst the tangled rings of self. Some of us here are historians seeking new knowledge—some wielding an ax, some a saw. The rest of us are histories seeking to be read, ready to be revealed by such tools.

Upstream, the People's Canal switches sides with the Aberdeen-Springfield, channeled ingeniously under. Prior to mechanization, mule teams walked the bank, dragging moss from the canals to prevent their clogging. Once, such a team fell in and was pulled under and through, emerging somewhat worse for the wear but alive. Soon after, screens were put in place to prevent any further recurrence.

History can pull just as strongly. We may one moment be sure of our perceptions and story, and the next be seeing it from a different perspective. We erect screens to prevent such swift changes, habits that keep us tethered to our timestream.

**

The local high school's hazing ceremony included a forced swim in the People's canal at the school year's end. The departing seniors rounded up the sophomores at lunch hour and hauled them to the People's, where they threw them in, clothes and all. Smallish and pre-pubescent, unable to even float, as a sophomore I dreaded the event yearlong, and on the rumored day of the event I left class early. I walked through two miles of grain and potato fields, staying far from the road and the seniors, to the neighboring town of Thomas, avoiding probable death and certain embarrassment.

Nothing can embarrass me here at Joe's, where we accept each other's habits and fears. I buy Johnny a beer. He puts a quarter on the foosball table to challenge the present game's winner. Stoned, drunk—swimming here is easy, though emerging from the current seems next to impossible. Here Kant and I agree—certain habits are nigh insurmountable.

It is not so much what you believe in that matters, as the way in which you believe it and proceed to translate that belief into action.
   --Lin Yutang, *The Importance of Living*

PACKING FOR NAIVETE: A FORAY INTO THE CRIMINAL MIND

Growing up in the penumbra of the Vietnam War and nearing its center as I reached draft age, I undertook a journey of naïveté, following the new generation of idealists. Scrawny, weak and yielding, possessing little, I was no challenger to those fearing for their place, no prey for those seeking coup, and to those wishing status by overcoming another I had no value. Making myself nothing, I could walk through small danger without suffering its consequence.

Inspired by what now seem naïve models, the westernized Buddhist images of Kung Fu and Siddhartha, I aimed to leave material culture. I turned off the television and radio, refusing membership with the broader community, instead began belonging, I believed, to all humanity and all creatures. My hair grew provocatively long, resisting style and conservative impositions. I altered my diet, making evident that I was psychologically abandoning my Western rural upbringing.

Leaving the Bucket

I refused to sign up for the draft, readied myself for jail. Moving my waking hours to the night, I shifted my attention to piercing the veils of the world. When I had to work, I worked the most lowly jobs—pipe moving, rock picking—alongside the illegal Mexican laborers pouring into the area, and I shared my vehicle with them when farmers' forced them to ride in the backs of their pickups. Reaching the age of legal drinking, I found that in my movements through subcultures that—to me, at least—the biker, the old-timer, the Indian, had the same status as the rich, the landed, the beautiful.

"He who would be friends with God," Gandhi wrote, "must remain alone, or make the whole world his friend." I moved through iniquity alone, assembled companions only briefly, as they randomly came. To do otherwise, to associate myself with any particular group, would be to exclude others. Nonetheless, in the world of Dionysus I found all to be amiable, everyone my friend. "Be self-indulgent," wrote Sartre, "and those who are also self-indulgent will like you." With a beer or a joint in hand, companions are not difficult to find.

On a long trek taken alone, the contents of one's pack must be capable of diversity, and there are few things as diverse as nothing—"never," writes Kierkegaard, "does reflection catch its prey so surely as when it makes its snare out of nothing." Lao-Tse, too, reminds us of the importance of emptiness as seen in the cup, as a hub of a wheel, as a window for our home. Nothing, in the realm of plenty, both signals that its wearer is no threat and draws in like a whirlpool what is needed.

Leaving preconceptions like carrion aside my path, I yet clung to a single possession—the belief that natural man was good—with which I intended to expose the illusory world. It would require a great number of incidents to break down that belief, to destroy the well-earned epiphanies with which I long supported it.

**

Long past one in the morning, the bar is closing. But even after twelve hours of imbibing the party feels to have just begun. Ida turns out the bar lights, hoping to discourage any passing police, and shuts down the stereo, trying to push the customers out as we buy cases of beer to go. A few of us linger, searching for the host of an after hours party. We decide upon Robert's, a biker living over twenty miles away.

The cars have been warming up and we've stocked up on beer. We follow Robert's taillights across the icy backroads—down lonely Ferry Butte Road, across the Snake River and the Reservation. We meet a set of oncoming lights with dread, knowing it may be the police, as we cut across the backside of Blackfoot, the only town. After turning down a side road, we head again away from town, this time toward the foothills, and pull into the driveway of a shack.

The house hasn't been painted for decades. Its fence lies in ruin and some of its windows are boarded.

Inside, however, the biker's girlfriend retains some of her mother's homemaking instructions, having created a livable space. Macramé, black light posters, lesser antiques and crafts adorn the cracked plaster walls. Robert cranks up the stereo, starts a fire in the woodstove, and we all open beers while he rolls a joint.

I head for the record collection, thumb through the vast numbers. Cream, Robin Trower, Yardbirds—I pause at Crosby, Stills, Nash and Young's *Déjà Vu*. Robert, observing my choice, shakes his head and calls me a "peace creep."

We drink beer, smoke dope, listen to music in the dim light and smoky haze. After an hour we split into small groups, and in another hour most have left, the beer dissipated. Robert breaks open the liquor cabinet, as we die-hards pair off into smaller units, coaxing from each other what interests us.

I engage a biker whom I have never met in a discussion of human nature, me asserting, him denying, that man is good. He thinks me naïve, I think him the same, each of us assuming the other to be a product of faulty conditioning. I forget the particulars of the lengthy argument—no doubt we recapitulated in bastardized form the arguments of philosophers who similarly disagree—but I recall believing I had convinced him with my rhetoric, after seeing the sun rise to end my day.

A day later the local paper's front page blares that a man had kidnapped his ex-wife and their two year old child—both of whom live just two miles from me—and hidden them in a cave on the Arco desert, where temperatures reached well below zero overnight. Unfamiliar with the man's name which others at the bar seem to know, I ask Ida to put a face to it—it is the biker I naively spoke with the night before.

**

Naïve then, I am perhaps as naïve now—and as self-centered, two decades later, believing the kidnapper was with his crime continuing our discussion, with an emphatic last word aiming to temper my belief. Searching for a reply I try to unpack his behavioral statement, but after great difficulty can only say, "Yes, you insist that man is bad."

That reason always falls to the blunt edge of action—of my despair over this I can barely speak. Faith, belief, and hope seem just primitive tools used as shelter from the truth: one man's base insistence can shatter all ideals. I overcome this surmise only with difficulty, realizing that just as a physical act can shatter ideals, so can brief intuitions destroy the bindings of matter—men have through momentary epiphanies salvaged entire lives devoted to evil, uplifting them into the world of spirit.

John Tallmadge describes one such small epiphany, incurred on a Great Basin trek: "the sense of remoteness hit me like the gut-cramping taste of cold spring water. Always before I had traveled in better-known wilderness areas, with maintained trails and rangers on patrol. If you got hurt, you could always count on someone coming along. But here we were completely cut off from the human world. It would be easy to die unheard of and unpitied. Perhaps I should have been nervous, but I felt more exhilarated than afraid. Standing amid the ruined temple rocks with a vast landscape flowing away on all sides, I felt as if I had reached the center of the world."

Such lucidity often arises in remoteness, after layers of civilization—prejudice, habit, desire—have been shed. Monks undertake pilgrimages intent on such process, hoping to break the shackles of physical existence. But like moments can even occur randomly, as we witness in Dostoevsky's *The Idiot*, in which the naïve Prince Myshkin finds lucidity in the seconds before his epileptic fits—a condition the author suffered. "In the midst of sadness, spiritual darkness and oppression," Dostoevsky writes, "there seemed at moments a flash of light in his brain, and with extraordinary impetus all his vital forces suddenly began working at their highest tension. The sense of life, the consciousness of self, were multiplied ten times at these moments which passed like a flash of lightning. His mind and his heart were flooded with extraordinary light; all his uneasiness, all his doubts, all his anxieties were relieved at once; they were all merged in a lofty calm, full of serene, harmonious joy and hope...He (later) often said to himself that all these gleams and flashes of the highest sensation of life and self-consciousness...were nothing but disease, the interruption of the normal condition; and if so, it was not at all the highest form of being, but on the contrary must be reckoned the lowest."

Epiphanies break the shackles of normalcy, but do they reveal a higher or a more base existence underlying the everyday? And if those of spirit aim for confirmation of their beliefs, might not those followers of the material world aim similarly toward epiphanies which prop up theirs?

**

I am the only Caucasian left at the Grandview bar. Joe Rojas, the owner and a second-generation immigrant, is the only other English-speaker present. Local farmers outnumber their Mexican help here during the day, but as the sun goes down the "wetbacks" trickle in, their evening sets of pipelines finally moved. Having just begun feeling my oats, I am inclined to stay where sensation remains fresh, though all my countrymen have left.

With our boss headed home, Margarito and I sit at the bar taking turns buying beers, and with each round my inadequate Spanish flows more freely. "Tongue more loose," he jokes, insisting I drink another. I comply.

With missing syntax and stabs at words with poor pronunciation, we recount the events of the lives we share, speak to the people with whom we work. Our gestures wide and vigorous, we laugh and agree, our wish to understand overwhelming our actual understanding.

A young Mexican whom I do not know stands beside me at the bar, orders a beer for us both. Turning to thank him, I place my hand on my knee, and he steps toward me, rubs his crotch against my hand. I ignore the gesture as accidental, too naïve to understand he is likely gay.

One of the laborers pulls out a guitar and sings mellowly, with a voice as fine as hundreds who have gained a fame he never will. Others trill their yells randomly between songs, releasing the weight of a long day of manual labor. I raise my beer to them, try to copy their vigor, they happily return the gesture—perhaps thinking I'm an "idiot" like Myshkin.

The yells die down near closing time, when suddenly an out-of-towner, large by Mexican scale, grabs another man by the throat and begins choking him. Joe grabs a baseball bat from beneath the bar, clubs the man again and again but he won't go down. Joe strikes him harder and harder. Two other men cling to the perpetrator's neck, trying to break his chokehold on the victim. He finally releases the man, staggering away. As blood streams down the man's face, I go outside to the pay phone to summon the police. The Mexican clientele scrambles for their cars, not wishing to risk deportation. An hour later, after the police have come and filed their report, I find Emilio, one of our workers, still hiding on the floor in the back of my car.

**

Without language the mind is a wild place, just perceptions of objects and intuition, as close to raw nature, perhaps, as most of us might ever come. Drinking, sex, the bodily functions, laughter, violence—every Dionysian festival seems to end this way, in a chaos of physical and sub-mental entities trying to occupy the same space.

"Nature is a fine mistress," Emerson wrote, rejecting John Muir's invitation to stay in wild Yosemite, "but a poor wife." Though he tried to restore value to wilderness, finding beauty if not art in nature, Emerson's interest was more genteel in character. He saw man's nature as inhabiting both physical and mental planes, and a mind unsullied by man's prejudice and mental mistakes could return to a natural, beautiful state just as a wilderness might be restored by proper stewardship.

The highest form of art is often the simplest, the most naïve, the artist's culture first absorbed, then discarded to reveal the beauty of the natural and the wild. The artist, the babe of lucid intention and the sage of great wisdom sometimes seem to share a simple, naïve vision, but between them lies a long, circuitous path, reaching from bodily knowledge to spiritual understanding, neither of which by itself can apprehend man's complete nature. The Upanishads addresses this false dichotomy: "To darkness are they doomed who worship only the body, and to greater darkness they who worship only the spirit… Those who worship both the body and the spirit, by the body overcome death, and by the spirit achieve immortality." The epiphanies of the soul tempt us to leave our physical nature, just as physical raptures pull us from spirit. Constructing ourselves as opposites, we must suffer constant rending—be criminal or saint, and troubled in our experiences between the two poles.

Leaving the Bucket

**

My companion has secured female coup for the night, and I have been only semi-conscious for some time. Rather than sit up front with them and feel my lack of physical partner, I choose to ride on the pickup bed beneath the protective camper shell. They help me into the back and close the tailgate. Grateful, I lie down, remote from social sensation.

The bed's iron ribs grate against my bones, the smell of dust, hay leaves and oil hangs heavy in the air. I shift, find a place where the air is breatheable, listen to the road as we head home.

As we peel from the parking lot, I am thrown from side to side. I can feel the rear end's torque lifting the bed. We swerve, speed, there is gravel spraying—we have left the highway and struck the shoulder of the road somewhere in the twenty five miles between town and home.

Though my companion drives recklessly, I do not worry—I can do nothing. My life is literally in his hands. This is peace, albeit a sad one, of impotence and invisibility—without body, I am without responsibility, without burden of doing or having. No point in time must be added to the present, I am here, now, can only be here, now.

I ponder this as I hear the long miles of highway, then the gravel, sense the turn, smell the dust. The pickup stops. We've reached my home—I have lived through another night.

Drawn forth to the physical world, my stark lucidity dissipates. I stagger out, open the house, crawl into bed, moving slowly so as not to get sick. As I reach toward sleep the girl's cries leap from the living room floor—he is plunging deep inside her, driving home the most vivid truth.

**

Alcohol—appropriately though rarely called "spirits"—can separate the mind from the body, allowing the user to reside first in one, then the other. Its addictive nature *we* provide: a naïve desire to halve ourselves, a desire that spawns the suffering addiction entails.

In Buddhist doctrine, all suffering is founded on similar desires. A rich prince naively isolated from the world's evils, the Buddha first encountered suffering, illness and death on an unauthorized trip outside his palace. Though shocked when his peaceful and beautiful world was shattered by the presence of decay, he did not turn from his wretched vision as most of us would, instead rejected his wealth for a lifetime of impoverished wandering. For decades he searched for an answer to the troubling question of omnipresent suffering, until one day he was struck with the answer: if one ceases desiring, one ceases suffering. Many interpret his message of renunciation as an instruction to quit feeling, though compassion is the overarching premise of Buddhist thought and practice.

Leaving the Bucket

Voltaire portrayed a similar process, an idyllic world deteriorating, in his classic satire *Candide*, in which the ultra-idealistic protagonist, after suffering an unbelievable series of rebukes to his belief that life is "the best of all possible worlds"—war, earthquakes, his mentor's immorality—tenuously clasps to life at the novel's end by "cultivating his garden". Candide's crippled grasp is one of small proportions, holding to a small plot of land in a finite time frame, unlike his lofty ideals which raced ahead to excite, tempt and ultimately destroy his psyche. Voltaire's message might seem the complement of the Buddha's: quit thinking and believing in lofty thoughts.

Candide's garden, Buddha's cessation of desire—answers not wholly unlike, answers to the emphatic crimes of physical and mental existence. Both Buddha and Candide begin their quests naïve, and in some sense end in a similar place, a part of the world renounced by a self more minute and composed.

To be naïve is to be artless, simple or natural, according to the Oxford English Dictionary, suggesting as much of art as of naïveté. Emerson called nature the "essences unchanged by man," and art the "mixture of (man's) will with the same things." A natural man, a man unchanged by man, would be a naïve man, without culture—artless. An unthinking man like Candide would perhaps be such a man, as might be one without desire, such as the Buddha.

**

The Mexicans arrived just two days ago, and the border patrol has already picked them up. Normally we would take this in stride, it being common for the help to be deported, only to return undaunted just days later. But this year Congress has passed a bill legalizing those workers who have come back year after year. Chon and Chuy qualify by its standards, so they are being illegally deported.

I get on the phone to a paralegal at a nonprofit legal organization, who insists we are within our rights to have the two detained so they can remain here. Naively believing his advice, we drive to the American Falls jail, where Immigration is holding the two laborers.

We explain their legal status to the agents, who refuse to listen, and my consequent anger only elicits theirs. "If we let them up here they'll take American jobs," the most vociferous one insists, staring tensely. After nearly an hour of haggling we give up, having little legal experience or power, expecting Chuy and Chon to return within the week.

But two days later armed officers with flak jackets come to the farm, confiscate the family van. Upset that their authority was questioned, they coerced the two laborers into signing false statements claiming that my brother-in-law drove them up from the border. The INS holds the van as evidence, an alleged instrument of the illegal act of smuggling workers and a final retort to the argument over the workers' legality.

For months the lawyers and judges bicker, while Chuy and Chon are held on a farm outside of Boise, unpaid for the work they do. After a year, Immigration returns the van, dismissing all charges so long as the incident is not revealed publicly.

**

Faced with such repeated experience, where might makes right, maintaining naïveté became increasingly difficult. Few believers remain wholehearted once confronted by opposing evidence. Dionysians, their festivals inevitably ending in violence, soon lose their lust for unstructured joy, its eventual yielding to chaos. Just as few Apollonian believers stay true when they see the security of overly plotted lives giving way to stale order. Many still insist they are full believers, however, unable to embrace the ambiguity of disbelief.

Those who do admit disbelief face a crisis of uncertainty and often undertake pilgrimages to clarify their vision. The Dionysian binge, the monkish retreat, is intended to confirm the believer's foundations. A kidnapper, an INS agent, someone naïve and intent on maintaining naivete, can with a punctuating act prove his beliefs true, restoring a semblance of security. Empowering the self, when the self is tied to a belief system, empowers the belief, which in turn empowers the self.

A believer's quest can be of small or great magnitude, and need not be into a vast physical wilderness. He can instead walk into the equally wild perimeters of society, or wander into the denied areas of the mind, the untidy places remote from what we consider the self. Wherever there is nature, there is frontier.

In a Mexican bar, in a biker's home, both frontiers to me, I sought a natural morality among what others considered society's debris. On hundreds of nights at distant hours, far from the seat of acknowledged religion, I sensed that morality, that beauty, that spirituality. And the aftermath of kidnappings and violence only slowly eroded my belief.

Only slowly did so, for when contrary evidence threatens our worldviews, we instinctively rush to protect them. Usually, rationalization suffices—with tautologies such as "it's God's will" or "it's human nature," we envelop such a broad array of paradoxes and contradictions that only long and labored reason can break their hold.

Our premises generate our actions. If I believe mankind inherently animal, I can justify my criminal impulses as natural, undeserving of punishment, guilt or remorse. If I accept the capitalist paradigm that selfishness is in everyone's best interest, I am allowed behavior which other societies under different sets of beliefs call criminal. I elevate what were once vices— usury and avarice—to virtue.

If we admit the converse to our premises, our lifework becomes a history of wrongdoing which we cannot face. We run from such truth. If evil appears in our religious world we pray to shore up our beliefs; if as capitalists we witness poverty we blame government intervention or the victims' lack of virtue; and when good appears in our criminal world, we may

Leaving the Bucket

commit a crime, showing the wrongness of opposing beliefs while restoring ours.

Crime can be a refuge, too, the only certainty its believers possess.

**

We have been drinking beer since early afternoon, have just finished a bottle of wine laced with cocaine. Tiring of each other's company, ready for new sensation, we go to a bar in Pocatello. *Blind Driver*, a bluegrass tinged acoustic band, has begun their set.

We find a table, order hard drinks. I scan the mostly empty tavern. The bouncer is a biker, six foot six of beard, muscle and tattoo. He sits at the door, taking cover charges to pay for the band. In the spirit of spontaneity, I cannot resist—I yell, "All you pussy bikers suck!"

Five foot eleven, one hundred fifty pounds, I have never taken a swing at someone in my life. My companions, though more physically able, are nonetheless mortified. I stare at the biker, who looks puzzledly back. Grinning stupidly but disarmingly, I walk over and introduce myself and buy him a beer. He shakes his head and calls me crazy. Between songs, we become drinking buddies, afterwards, friends.

**

Dostoevsky's Prince Myshkin describes himself: "My gestures are unsuitable. I've no right sense of proportion. My words are incongruous, not befitting the subject…" Sufficiently naïve, Myshkin is tolerated and loved, avoiding duels and danger only because of his straightforward, Jesus-like attributes. Others allow him to belong precisely because he is so strange and unthreatening that he doesn't.

Myshkin lacks the cunning and art of civilized living. When he leaves Switzerland for Russia he has but a coin and a bundle, trusting the world to provide for his meager needs—which it does. Within days he is left a fortune, finding an awkward acceptance in Russian high society.

Dostoevsky's world was a better provider than I found mine to be.

One packs for an internal quest just as Myshkin prepared for his journey. Proper shoes, a change of clothes, a modicum of sustenance—the list differs according to the trek and he who takes it. The length of the journey must be considered, as does the extent of one's abilities. Tools which double in function, clothes suitable in many weathers, food unlikely to spoil—the objects more hardy, those most capable of diversity, are the most valuable in a pack's contents.

What one takes on a journey bears importance, but that left behind is as telling. A woman traveling the Orient with but a backpack does so with a different intent than the climber of Everest with a fax machine and a team of sherpas. The less culture we take, the more likely we will witness artless nature. The greatest spiritual journeys known are forays into nothingness, the pilgrim shedding layers of self as he nears it.

We think of "nothing" as designating emptiness, but Gregory Bateson often reminded readers that nothing can be something in the world of communication—the discovery of zero allowed mathematics a great advance, and a letter I don't send, a reply I don't make or a glance I refuse can all make a difference to others. What we don't carry with us, then, can tell those we encounter—and ourselves—a great deal, and one packs lightly on a trek toward naïveté.

Tallmadge forayed into the Deep Creek Mountains, a remarkable oasis-like range hidden in the Great Basin of Nevada and Utah. In the Deeps, insects and fish long extinct elsewhere survive the shrinking ecology of once enormous Lake Bonneville, which covered much of the West ten thousand years ago. Surrounding the Deeps is the old lake bed, now a desert lying parched and flat for hundreds of miles, without "sign of human life, not a road, not a building, not even a vapor trail in the sky." Tallmadge found a sort of purity in the anomalous Deeps and in himself, removed from the much more vast systems of society and desert. He was perhaps in the "fish-eye" of the yin-yang symbol, the opposite inside opposite inside unity. Once wholly in that eye we more easily see what we haven't, distance and distinction giving shape to what before evaded focus.

A naturalist can trek into the wilderness to find that distance, but inner, spiritual journeys require a space which has its reference only in mind. And the mind spreads distant, far broader than any wilderness or desert. What we sense internally is relation between the points most vivid upon the mind, which we name ideas or images, between where in our impressions we place ourselves and any other place upon which we focus. Though much like a great basin in its vastness, its features obey no physical laws—any journey across may either take years or occur instantly, depending as much upon the whim of synaptic fate as upon the quality of our will.

Physical places and objects can be touched, described, pointed out to others, but our internal images resist description. Attempting to do so is like describing color over the phone to a deaf and blind man—the objects in my mind may not correspond to those in yours; we may not give them the same names; their depth, their breadth, differs from mind to mind and are hidden from some, not from others.

We cannot therefore know exactly the objects in another's mind, but we can sense the pattern of placement in which they reside. Center, perimeter, penumbra—we sense these places as priorities in relation to others. Every concept and belief has a position, is a landmark, a priority, moving in conjunction with its relatives and its opposite. When we take drugs, we seek to shift these entrenched positions, and when we go mad from over-imbibing we have merely lost the relationships between our landmarks.

Marijuana smokers begin their habits as believers, their highs structured around observing the world in a different manner than the everyday. Minute details normally unseen, such as the neighbor's dog's idiosyncrasies, become absurd or acquire depth, as the worlds beneath the world take on prominence. Such multi-leveled experience may continue untroubling for years, until the moment when a smoker's attention wanders from the external world to himself. When he instead of the dog becomes funny and loses concreteness, he often succumbs to paranoia and a sickening hyper-self-consciousness. If his premises—his self—grow too shaky, he quits his habit.

**

Gregory Bateson believed alcoholism to be a cure for a particular "style of sobriety," and psychoanalyst Adam Phillips considered symptoms to be a sort of cure. When our beliefs fester—either their premises failing or the relationships between them giving way—our symptoms try to cure their ill state. A crime may restore those beliefs to a criminal, as might a punctuating epiphany to a saint.

Traditionally, American philosophy would judge those beliefs by how well they worked, and postmodernists would renege on the duty of judging them at all. But those seeking the higher ground of truth must use different criteria. It may very well be that all beliefs are equal, that man is at bottom neither good nor bad. Perhaps, even, there is no good or bad—just impressions of each, from a perspective embracing one or the other, depending in which eye of the yin-yang symbol we dwell. But if we choose between beliefs, we must surely prefer living as unburdened as do the naïve, and assume that man, at bottom, is good—even though we may suspect that the truly evil live just as lightly, having no weighty conscience to encumber them.

My questioning must thus aim less at the world than at myself, less "what is the world?" than "what am I?" and "how should I act within it?" Buckminster Fuller summarized one possible answer, suggesting that since pessimists denied the possible and optimists denied the real, only a realist could assimilate both.

Fuller, however, was optimistic about man's ability to assess reality. Idealists act upon belief, intentionally and foolishly so, but realists act on constructs they believe to be true, not knowing that they may in fact not be. A belief masked as fact, regardless of its truth, is surely more difficult to dismantle than one not shrouded.

Philosophers call the attitude that one can apprehend the world as it is "naïve realism," and use such evidence as subatomic physics, the delayed nature of sensory data and the subjectivity of color to dispute the view. But even these philosophers are guilty of naïveté, if they think these scientific arguments to be any more a description of the "real" than the naïve realist's.

Kidnapper, philosopher or idealist, we construct our worlds on premises that lend order to our lives, connect the thoughts and experiences in our minds in comprehensible ways. If we believe the world is fixed and act accordingly, we shrink the possibilities which dwell outside the parameters which we give it— precisely by the number of actions which we might have committed toward change, had we not adopted our fixed and constraining belief.

"Everything that looks to the future elevates human nature," wrote L.E. Landon, "for life is never so low or so little as when occupied with the present." If Jesus, Buddha and those yet following on the trek toward naïveté assessed reality and acted accordingly, they would not have undertaken improbable acts. That our actions may be futile, our goals unlikely to be reached, can make no difference in our decisions, lest we all become criminals, our worlds confined by the self intent on the survival of its beliefs.

FIRST DREAMS AND MUSTARD SEEDS

I must be between two and three years of age, for in my dream I can barely reach into my mother's sewing machine. I stand on my toes, swing the tray open, pull out a small metal bobbin wound with thread. I fondle the object as I return toward my crib, but almost immediately it begins gaining weight at a disturbing rate—infinitely so, until in but seconds it wholly engulfs my being with its mass. My toddler's gait slows, stops. I bend, stumble, weaken. The weight oppresses, sickens me, completely overtakes my will—and then I wake.

Some believe that a first dream sets the tone of the dreamer's life, being either an unconscious force that drives the future or a shorthand premonition describing what is destined. It is as though we come into the world as randomly rolling marbles, seeking the groove which the first dream provides. No doubt, early impressions color all those following and later experience will less likely muddy the strongest of them, so a powerful dream might indeed rule a dreamer's life—as a background crux for memory or emotion, or perhaps as a memento to be long fondled.

Small events in biological and social systems, according to Anthony Wilden, often have effects disproportionate to their size, for each subsequent event in the system's life can amplify or recursively affect the original cause. He writes, "a relatively small withdrawal of affection...in the first year of a human child's life can become amplified into relatively large psychological...changes in later life. Some...may prove to be irreversible." Accustomed to thinking of all causes as cue balls, we believe that striking another ball the same way with the same force will always end with the same result, but in systems comprised of self-willing agents, like actions rarely end with like outcomes. An event transpiring early in a system's life may reverberate throughout its history, though the same event repeated later may have little effect at all.

We are unpredictable systems, as prone to the effects of small events as large ones, but even if such a small occurrence as a first dream does not affect a future as dramatically as some believe, the enormous, incongruous gravity exerted by my tiny dream bobbin nonetheless would for me prove metaphorically correct—what should have been minute struggles in my hand would take on highly disproportionate mass, overwhelming and paralyzing me for the many years I held them.

**

It was from my mother's sewing machine that my dream-self removed the weighty bobbin, upon which her thread of suffering was tightly wound. That thread was strung from World War II Germany to a small desert community in Idaho, and tied what must be the fullest sensation of ego—the fascist, patriotic self wrapped up in its parent nation's world dominance—to the bombed out rubble and impoverished soul of the fallen and totally isolated.

Her family part of the German territory partitioned to Czechoslovakia after World War I, she grew up resentful, a second class citizen to the ruling Czechs. So when Hitler came to power simultaneously with her adulthood he was to some degree her savior, returning the German Czechs to their "rightful" status. She swiftly became part of the prosperous and rising Reich, moving up through the social ranks until she was working in the offices of one of Hitler's right-hand men, Saukel, who would eventually be hung at Nuremburg for his dealings with "foreign labor." Never joining the Nazi party, she nonetheless experienced the joy of belonging to the winning group, and she would experience as well the consequent losing, a long, drawn-out fall. Marrying my American father after the war, she was sentenced to a life as a rural housewife and mother—it was a long string of regrets over which she would not recover, one which as children we were reminded of often.

**

A crust of bread, a stolen sausage, the rubble of a home bombed. A dinner of nettles, a single stick of wood for warmth, the family and friends who would never come home—these were the German, wartime sufferings, but those which followed, in Idaho, seemed worse. The icy rooms of my grandparents' home, the chilled heart of my grandmother, the poverty of a rural desert. The snowdrifts high as telephone poles, the dry and oppressive summer heat when she lay pregnant on the cool cement floor, the loneliness of a woman exiled to the victor's homeland, the letter every few years telling of another family member dying, whose funeral we had not the money to allow her to attend— these facts hammered home my mother's despair. As American, as a part of the family which weighted her here, I felt as though I was somehow its cause.

**

Allan Young suggests there are two primary types of suffering. Physical pain can be suffered by any sufficiently evolved organism, but existential or psychical pain "has a social or moral dimension" experienced differently by different communities. Some groups deny their members psychical suffering, even though they may be as hurt as individuals in other groups that allow similar pain's expression. Even within the same culture, the members may articulate and experience pain differently.

Many cultures utilize suffering to solidify membership, so to give every minor grief hearing would trivialize their rituals' importance. The world's societies abound with painful rites—bodily mutilations, spiritual pilgrimages—intended to propel the sufferer to a higher level of existence or a deeper belonging. Such traditions, when authentic, consist of specific timing and meaning, are conducted in a context and spirit of readiness. The participant must be prepared for, not simply desire, higher status, must be granted exaltation rather than seize it.

Our occidental heroes are sufferers—Christ, Joan of Arc, Prometheus, Socrates—and to emulate them we too must suffer. In our times, the emphasis on suffering seems strengthened, while the transcendence which traditionally follows is ignored. Thus, our heroes are often anti-heroes: dead rock and rollers, James Dean characters—those who break, rather than transcend, rules or the status quo.

**

My mother milks the cows morning and night, summer and winter. A flour sack wraps her head to keep the manure from her pinned-up hair, felt lined women's boots feebly protect her feet from the cold. Even in thirty below weather, she must wash the cow's teats, the water soon freezing her bare hands. Every touch on metal pipes or wood or twine cracks her skin, and the bruises from kicking cows rise purple and yellow.

My father takes over briefly while she cooks us six children breakfast, and then she returns to milking for two more hours. During the day she bakes, cans, sews and gardens, paints our house on rickety scaffolding, milks cows again at night and then cooks supper. We help with other chores but she refuses to let us milk, not wishing her children to take the path which their parents have.

Often we seek martyrdom, and threatened to be deprived of our suffering we instead seek it, hold it closely rather than share it and unburden ourselves—relief from pain only lowers our martyr status.

**

A young idealist in the sixties, my heroes are artists, draft-dodgers, those willing to give up their lives for higher purposes—sufferers all. Taking seriously the deaths of both local and enemy soldiers, I grasp at what suffering I can, wanting to share in the overcoming of wrong. I protestingly grow my hair to shoulder length, inviting violence and ridicule from the highly conservative populace, become a vegetarian, believing every act of violence abandoned will make the world a better place. I refuse to register for the draft, risking jail.

Already a minority as a liberal minded non-Mormon, I increasingly enjoy the empowerment which self-righteousness brings. In thought, I stand against the establishment and all evil—what greater act, what more deserving of pride?

The draft ended the year of my call, so I was spared a confrontation with the government and a real test of my will and courage. And while the war ended, my disillusion remained. I drifted like millions of others toward the risen, Dionysian culture, and there continued the path of suffering I'd grown to love.

**

Love and death are the manna for most of man's psychical suffering—I grasp each eagerly as they come my way. Seventeen, I fall in love with a girl who but shows me a kindness and spend months in imaginary romance—though I do not so much as telephone her. I wait instead for hours in parking lots, along roads, at events, believing chance and the goodness of the universe will bring us together. I write bad poetry, dream, cry in despair and rejoice in hope.

Physically and emotionally isolated in a conservative, rural area, I was lonely, so fixed upon the least dangerous object to me—the mental construct of love and its attendant emotions. Harry Stack Sullivan wrote that it is "very difficult…to get anyone to remember clearly how he felt and what he did when he was horribly lonely." I can summarize my experience in but a paragraph, but not its depth, not its intensity—not its foolishness. Many may feel as strongly for small portions of their lives, few do so with so little reason to.

My suffering doubled when a close acquaintance was instantly killed in a car accident. I railed against God for the senseless occurrence—and for all death. I spent hours each day through a cold fall and winter at my friend's graveside, conversing with him in death as I had not in life.

Death, like imagined love, provides intensity without obvious risk. The perished and the beloved rarely reply.

In the Buddhist parable of the mustard seed, a monk is approached by a woman mad with grief over her son's death. He listens to her story, directs her to the nearby city where she is to go door to door, collecting grains of mustard seed from those homes where no one has died. After but a few visits she realizes there are no such homes, and utters this, returned to sanity: "No village law, no law of market town, No law of a single house is this—Of all the world and all the worlds of Gods This only is the Law, that all things are impermanent." Death is omnipresent, and our own suffering looms overwhelming only until we turn our attention to others'.

"Without mourning for primary objects," writes psychologist Adam Phillips, "there is no way out of the magic circle of family." Neither, he says, is there identity. A first death and a first love can propel one from family, and a first dream can shade the remainder of one's life. We only have to let them go to deprive them of their power, but without them what identity do we have?

**

"The present has no extension except in intensity," said Lama Anagarika Govinda. Loneliness strips the future and the past from experience, and in the changeless present there can be no information to convey—there is only more...more...more, like the multiplying mass of the bobbin.

Noted explorer Richard Byrd, in solitude for months at the South Pole on a meteorological mission, could not write of the intense aloneness he experienced there until years later, for language is shed from the mind embracing that emptiness. He wrote:

"….the effect of isolation on a man…is difficult for me to put…into words. I can only feel the absence of certain things, the exaggeration of others."

Byrd found that "absence of conversation makes it harder…to think in words. Sometimes, while walking, I talk to myself and listen to the words, but they sound hollow and unfamiliar. Today, for example, I was thinking of the extraordinary effect of the lack of diversions upon my existence; but describing it is beyond my power. I could feel the difference between this life and a normal life; I could see the difference in my mind's eye, but I couldn't satisfactorily express the subtleties in words. That may be because I have already come to live more deeply within myself; what I feel needs no further definition, since the senses are intuitive and exact."

At such deep moments of solitude we are in a world removed from the everyday, and to describe it with the language of normal life makes our experience pale. I cannot express how it was to be lonely for hours, days, months, consumed with love and death, to wake to despair each morning, wallow in pain all day, and finally stare deep into each night seeking—and at times finding—answers. Such a life just extends Govinda's present, fixed on a single emotion, bereft of language and its normalcy.

First the bobbin, then the loved, then the perished overwhelmed my being with disproportionate weight, and the thread spun upon them lay attached to the empty center of self.

**

There is some physiological evidence to suggest that victims become chemically "addicted" to their suffering. When traumatic memories are re-enacted, the body releases chemicals to alleviate them, and some think the desire to experience this release causes sufferers to recall their traumatic pasts in order to trigger it.

Young reiterates the Pavlovian belief that a victim can either respond to such memory by developing routines to avoid the noxious stimuli or by giving up. But he also posits a third possibility, one arising in connection with posttraumatic stress disorder: victims of traumatic memory can seek replication of those events.

According to Young, anecdotal and experimental evidence suggest that endorphins enter a victim's bloodstream during traumatic shock. The endorphins allow a victim to either continue fleeing or fighting danger, undeterred by pain. Afterward, upon repeated recall of the events, the sufferers of post traumatic stress become addicted both to the endorphins and to the memories that release them.

**

The addict winds his life around a central object, usually his suffering. That suffering for me is the emptiness at the bobbin's center, loneliness. My days encircle the spool, passing identical axes—the withdrawal, the first drink, the engulfment and loss of self, loss of consciousness, withdrawal, first drink...-

-without end. I may go to different places, meet different people, but still I am circling the same hub of my disease.

A tormented Kierkegaard, who for a lifetime suffered the process of loneliness, wrote: "To wish to break down my self-isolation by continually thinking of breaking it down leads to the directly opposite result." Thought reinforces the cycle which only action can break, embedding it more deeply in the sufferer.

Kierkegaard, much like an addict clinging to habit, chose to retain his lifelong solitude, though he had within immediate reach the ready possibility of redemption. A woman loved him dearly—and he refused her. He was offered profession, which he declined. He must have loved, even while hating, his suffering—as do most of us embroiled in addiction.

**

After several months my dead friend appears in a dream, vampire-like and haggard, warning me away. Soon after, my fictitious love marries a missionary for whom two years she has waited. I receive the messages as rejections, a further push into despair.

From mental to physical phenomena—my cycle of self-incurred suffering, now a way of life well-practiced, turns from idea to substance, years at the local tavern. During these years I am still lonely, carrying the ideals of the sixties, the ideas of the humanists, amid a people concerned only with survival and sensation.

Leaving the Bucket

I have learned to be a minority: my mother a German in America, our family non-Mormons in a Mormon community, me an intellectual in a people of body, of hands. Were I to find a like mind I would likely reject it, so versed I am in my solitude.

The years pass on like the eras before, gain only in intensity and not difference. Now, the further those years recede, the less I can recall the pleasure which drew me to drink. I remember instead the wake of those addictive sensations, the hangovers, racked with psychic pain—

I can barely walk to the refrigerator, drink from a pitcher of orange juice. Trembling, my head spinning, I stumble back to bed. My body is weak. My mind races between remorse over last night's foolhardiness and self-mortification over past mistakes. To escape, I fix my attention on possible pleasures. I imagine myself with someone distant whom I might love. But the mental does not satisfy. I touch myself, let those sensations overwhelm the pain of both past and present. But after ejaculation there is only more remorse—part of another addiction, another desire attempting satiety but only creating more desire.

I try to sleep, but can only wallow in emotion, wish for change but not act toward it. Desirous but helpless, penitent and regretful but unable to make amends, I fight the illness I have imposed on myself. I masturbate again, ending one desire, but it rises an hour later to be quelled again. I bathe, seeking cleanliness, but my sweat fills with methanol, stains my skin and hair. Hunger, thirst—a piece of toast, a cold drink of juice, a weary fall back to bed. A need for sensation—a cool part of the sheets, a soft ply of velvet, my hand on myself, imagining another. Silence, distant silence. Overwrought with embarrassment and shame.

By afternoon the crowding sensations wane somewhat, but the empty loneliness which appears seems somehow worse. Here the battle begins anew: I can end the stifling nothingness by driving up to the bar, or spend the next several hours—and a subsequent night of uneasy sleep—wrestling with dis-ease.

Three months into Byrd's Antarctic trial, he succumbed to monoxide poisoning due to an improperly functioning heater. Too weak to repair the heater, he found himself in a tricky situation: if he left it off he would freeze to death or die of thirst (he had to melt food and ice on the stove to provide his sustenance), and if he left it on he would eventually poison himself.

Feebly wavering between the two alternatives, Byrd struggled to maintain his life as he sat alone, unwilling and perhaps unable to be saved by his companions at Little America, a base nearly two hundred miles away. He wrote: "I sank to depths of disillusionment which I had not believed possible. It would be tedious to discuss them. Misery, after all, is the tritest of emotions. All that need be said is that eventually my faith began to make itself felt; and by concentrating on it and reaffirming the truth about the universe as I saw it, I was able again to fill my mind with the fine and comforting things of the world that had seemed irretrievably lost. I surrounded myself with my family and my friends; I projected myself into the sunlight, into the midst of green, growing things. I thought of all the things I would do when I got home…But time after time slipped back into despond. Concentration was difficult, and only by the utmost persistence could I bring myself out of it…"

Byrd wrestled with calling for help for weeks, as he spent his weakened hours crawling from storehouse to stove to bed in tiny increments of spent energy. Afterwards, he reasoned elaborately that he refused to summon help so his fellow men wouldn't be endangered, but it could easily be argued that a Kierkegaardian pride kept him from asking for help. Whether we are wounded animals hiding our pain so we might escape further injury, or stricken egos admitting our mortality and dependency on others, we often hold to our suffering and extend it rather than sharing and thus transcending it.

The process of Byrd's justifiable despondency—he was, after all, suffering weather of fifty below zero in a land of total darkness, with a condition approaching death—was mimicked by my own shallow, if real, despair. Poisoned, we both reached for the good things in our life but failed to reach them, as we crawled from bed to sustenance and back, simultaneously trying to survive and hoping we wouldn't.

**

In the story "The Button," a man confined to solitary imprisonment rips a button from his shirt and tosses it into the darkness of his cell in order to maintain his sanity. He then spends the rest of the day finding it, thus ingenuously enabling him to evade monotony. Morning after morning he throws the button, spends the day finding it again. But one day he tosses it and cannot find it, and he goes increasingly mad as he searches and searches the finite floor of the cell. Unable to find the button, he dies—it has caught in a spider's web above him.

We perhaps all need such a button to attend to, a bobbin to spin our lives upon. Hopeful or weighty, talismans as varied as drugs, love, death and solitude provide meaning in a life doomed otherwise to emptiness. We can love, or love the idea of love; cling to all the trappings of loneliness, even when we despise experiencing it.

At the level of subatomic string theory, particles can "borrow" mass of infinitely great proportion so long as they quickly return it. Small sufferings, too, can lease intensity from greater ones. In my first dream in memory I was returning to the crib with a borrowed bobbin of overwhelming mass, and now I return that suffering to my mother's sewing machine, give back to her what I had earlier taken.

I am free.

BIBLIOGRAPHY

Barrett, William. *The Illusion of Technique*. New York: Doubleday, 1979.

Bateson, Gregory . *Steps to an Ecology of Mind*. Ballantine Books, New York, 1972. Reprinted with a foreword by Mary Catherine Bateson, University of Chicago Press, 2000.

Bateson, Gregory. *Mind and Nature: A Necessary Unity*. Ballantine Books, New York, 1979.

Bateson, Gregory & Mary Catherine. *Angels Fear*. Macmillan, New York, 1987.

Byrd, Richard Evelyn. *Alone*. Washington, D.C. Island Press, 2003.

Flemons, Douglas. *Completing Distinctions*. Boston, MA: Shambhala Publications, 1991.

Fromm, Erich. *Anatomy of Human Destructiveness*. New York: Holt, Rinehart and Winston, 1973.

Liebow, Elliot. *Talley's Corner, A Study of Negro Streetcorner Men*. Boston: Little, Brown, 1967.

Phillips, Adam. *On Kissing, Tickling, and Being Bored: Psychoanalytic Essays on the Unexamined Life.* Cambridge, Mass.: Harvard University Press, 1993.

Phillips, Adam. *Terrors and Experts.* Cambridge, Mass.: Harvard University Press, 1996.

Phillips, Adam. *Beast in the Nursery.* New York: Pantheon Books, c1998.

Phillips, Adam. *Darwin's Worms.* London: Faber, 1999.

Rawlins, C.L. *Sky's Witness: A Year in the Wind River Range.* New York: Holt, 1993.

Rappaport, Roy A. *Ecology, Meaning and Religion.* Richmond, Calif.: North Atlantic Books, 1973.

Sluzki, Carlos E. and Donald C. Ransom, Editors. *Double Bind: The Foundation of the Communicational Approach to the Family.* New York: Grune & Stratton; London: distributed in the United Kingdom by Academic Press, 1976.

Tallmadge, John. *Meeting the Tree of Life: A Teacher's Path.* University of Utah Press, 1967.

Tyler, Anne. *The Accidental Tourist*. New York: Knopf, 1985.

Waldrop, Mitchell M. *Complexity: The Emerging Science at the Edge of Order and Chaos*. New York: Touchstone, 1992.

Wilden, Anthony. *The Rules Are No Game: The Strategy of Communication*. New York: Routledge & Kegan Paul, 1987.

Young, Allan. *The harmony of Illusions: Inventing Post-traumatic Stress Disorder*. Princeton, N.J.: Princeton University Press, 1995.

ABOUT THE AUTHOR

Ralph Thurston writes reflective non-fiction from his five acre cut flower farm in Blackfoot, Idaho, where he lives and works with his wife and inspiration, watercolorist Jeriann Sabin. His essays have been published in such diverse publications as *Growing For Market* and *The Georgia Review*, and his most recent effort, *No Sage: Essays From the Margin*, which wove its way around his work as farmer, trapper, and apiarist in a rapidly changing Southeast Idaho, was a finalist for the 2002 Idaho Book Award.